W9-BBA-053

中国国家汉办赠送
Donated by Hanban, China

Wise Men Talking Series

ZHUANG ZI
庄子说 Says 蔡希勤 编注

□ 责任编辑 **韩晖**

□ 翻译 **王琴 姜防震**

□ 绘图 **李士伋**

华语教学出版社

SINOLINGUA

First Edition   2006

ISBN 7 – 80200 – 213 – 3
Copyright 2006 by Sinolingua
Published by Sinolingua
24 Baiwanzhuang Road, Beijing 100037, China
Tel: (86)10 – 68995871
Fax: (86)10 – 68326333
Website: www. sinolingua. com. cn
E – mail: hyjx@ sinolingua. com. cn
Printed by Beijing Songyuan Printing Co. Ltd.
Distributed by China International
Book Trading Corporation
35 Chegongzhuang Xilu, P. O. Box 399
Beijing 100044, China

Printed in the People's Republic of China

俗曰:"不听老人言,吃亏在眼前。"

老人家走的路多,吃的饭多,看的书多,经的事多,享的福多,受的罪多,可谓见多识广,有丰富的生活经验,老人家说的话多是经验之谈,后生小子不可不听也。

在中国历史上,春秋战国时期是中国古代思想高度发展的时期,那个时候诸子并起,百家争鸣,出现了很多"子"字辈的老人家,他们有道家、儒家、墨家、名家、法家、兵家、阴阳家,多不胜数,车载斗量,一时星河灿烂。

后来各家各派的代表曾先后聚集于齐国稷下学宫,齐宣王是个开明的诸侯王,因纳无盐丑女钟离春为后而名声大噪,对各国来讲学的专家学者不问来路一律管吃管住,享受政府津贴,对愿留下来做官的,授之以客卿,造巨室,付万钟。对不愿做官的,也给予"不治事而议论"之特殊待遇。果然这些人各为其主,各为其派,百家争鸣,百花齐放,设坛辩论,著书立说:有的说仁,有的说义,有的说无为,有的说逍遥,有的说非攻,有的说谋攻,有的说性善,有的说性恶,有的说亲非亲,有的说马非马,知彼知已,仁者无敌……留下了很多光辉灿烂的学术经典。

可惜好景不长,秦始皇时丞相李斯递话说"焚书坑儒",结果除秦记、医药、卜筮、种树书外,民间所藏诗、书及百家典籍一把火烧个精光。到西汉武帝时,董仲舒又上了个折子,提出"罢黜百家,独尊儒术",从此,儒学成了正统,"黄老、刑名百家之言"成为邪说。

"有德者必有言",儒学以外的各家各派虽屡被扫荡,却不断变幻着生存方式以求不灭,并为我们保存下了十分丰富的经典著作。在这些经典里,先哲们留下了很多充满智慧和哲理的、至今仍然熠熠发光的至理名言,我们将这些各家各派的老人家的"金玉良言"编辑成这套《老人家说》丛书,加以注释并译成英文,采取汉英对照出版,以飨海内外有心有意于中国传统文化的广大读者。

As the saying goes, "If an old dog barks, he gives counsel."

Old men, who walk more roads, eat more rice, read more books, have more experiences, enjoy more happiness, and endure more sufferings, are experienced and knowledgeable, with rich life experience. Thus, what they say is mostly wise counsel, and young people should listen to them.

The Spring and Autumn (722 – 481 BC) and War-ring States (475 – 221 BC) periods of Chinese history were a golden age for ancient Chinese thought. In those periods, various schools of thought, together with many sages whose names bore the honorific suffix "Zi", e-merged and contended, including the Taoist school, Confucian school, Mohist school, school of Logicians, Legalist school, Military school and Yin-Yang school. Numerous and well known, these schools of thought were as brilliant as the Milky Way.

Later representatives of these schools of thought flocked to the Jixia Academy of the State of Qi. Duke Xuan of Qi was an enlightened ruler, famous for making an ugly but brilliant woman his empress. The duke pro-vided board and lodging, as well as government subsi-dies for experts and scholars coming to give lectures, and never inquired about their backgrounds. For those willing to hold official positions, the duke appointed them guest officials, built mansions for them and paid them high salaries. Those unwilling to take up official posts were kept on as advisors. This was an era when "one hundred schools of thought contended and a hundred flowers blossomed." The scholars debated in forums, and wrote books to expound their doctrines: Some preached benevolence; some, righteousness; some, inaction; some, absolute freedom; some, aversion to offensive war; some, attack by stratagem; some, the goodness of man's nature; some, the evil nature of man. Some said that relatives were not relatives; some said that horses were not horses; some urged the importance of knowing oneself and one's enemy; some said that benevolence knew no enemy... And they left behind many splendid classic works of scholarship.

Unfortunately, this situation did not last long. When Qin Shihuang (reigned 221 – 206 BC) united all the states of China, and ruled as the First Emperor, his prime minister, Li Si, ordered that all books except those on medicine, fortune telling and tree planting be burned. So, all poetry collections and the classics of the various schools of thought were destroyed. Emperor Wu (reigned 140 – 88 BC) of the Western Han Dynasty made Confucianism the orthodox doctrine of the state, while other schools of thought, including the Taoist and Legalist schools, were deemed heretical.

These other schools, however, managed to survive, and an abundance of their classical works have been handed down to us. These classical works contain many wise sayings and profound insights into philosophical theory which are still worthy of study today. We have compiled these nuggets of wisdom uttered by old men of the various ancient schools of thought into this series Wise Men Talking, and added explanatory notes and English translation for the benefit of both Chinese and overseas readers fond of traditional Chinese culture.

目录

CONTENTS

伯夷死名于首阳之下〔10〕
Bo Yi died for his reputation on Mount Shouyang...

不利货财，不近贵富〔12〕
He will not crave for property and wealth and will not strive for fame and position.

不忘其所始，不求其所终〔14〕
The true man in ancient times did not forget the origin of his life; he did not explore the final destiny of his life.

C

蝉方得美阴而忘其身〔16〕
A cicada had just found a fine spot in the shade and ignored the imminent danger.

长者不为有余，短者不为不足〔18〕
The long is not to be considered too much and the short is not to be considered too little.

唇竭则齿寒〔20〕
Since the lips are gone, the teeth get cold...

D

大声不入于里耳〔22〕

Grand music will not appeal to the villagers.

道不可闻，闻而非也〔24〕
As Tao cannot be heard, what can be heard is not Tao.

道行之而战，物谓之而然〔26〕
A path is formed because we walk on it; a thing has a name
because we call it so.

德有所长，而形有所忘〔28〕
For men with ample virtue, their physical defects might be
forgotten.

E

儿子终日嗥而嗌不嗄〔30〕
A new-born baby can cry all day without losing its voice because
it is in the perfection of equilibrium.

F

夫大壑之为物也〔32〕
The vast sea is something you cannot fill by pouring in water and
you cannot drain up by drawing water.

夫富者，苦身疾作〔34〕
Men of wealth toil and moil to accumulate more riches than they

can possibly consume.

夫鹄不日浴而白〔36〕
The swans are white although they do not bathe themselves every day...

夫水行不避蛟龙者，渔父之勇也〔38〕
To travel by the water in defiance of the flood dragons shows the valour of the fishermen...

夫天地至神，而有尊卑先后之序〔40〕
If the Heaven and the Earth, which are the most sacred, have their distinction of rank and order...

夫昭昭生于冥冥〔42〕
Brightness originates from darkness.

G

狗不以善吠为良〔44〕
As a dog is not considered good merely because it barks well...

古之所谓得志者，非轩冕之谓也〔46〕
By "fulfillment of ambition," the men of ancient times did not mean obtaining high ranks of office...

古之畜天下者，无欲而天下足〔48〕

In ruling over the world in ancient times, the kings enriched the world by having no desires.

古之至人，先存诸己而后存诸人〔50〕

The perfect men in the past saw to it that they had Tao in themselves before they passed it on to others.

官施而不失其宜〔52〕

The sage places his officials in appropriate positions, and promotes his officials according to their talents.

观之名则不见，求之利则不得〔54〕

He owns nothing in terms of possession and fame.

H

何谓道？有天道，有人道〔56〕

What do we mean by Tao? There is the Tao in the natural way and there is the Tao in the human way.

虎之与人异类，而媚养己者，顺也〔58〕

The tiger is of a different species from man, yet it is gentle to its keeper because the keeper complies with its disposition.

惠子谓庄子曰（无用之用）〔60〕

Hui Zi said to Zhuang Zi, "Your words are useless."

惠子相梁，庄子往见之〔62〕

When Hui Zi became the prime minister in the State of Liang,
Zhuang Zi was going to see him.

祸福淳淳〔64〕

Good fortune and bad fortune have their comings and goings...

J

鉴明则尘垢不止〔66〕

There is no dust on a bright mirror while a dusty mirror is not
bright.

今且有人于此（随侯之珠）〔68〕

If a man is now shooting with a precious pearl at a sparrow
flying high in the sky, he will surely be laughed at.

金石有声，不考不鸣〔70〕

Though musical instruments may give sounds, they will not
ring unless they are struck.

井蛙不可以语于海者〔72〕

You cannot discuss the sea with a frog at the bottom of a well...

鸡鸣狗吠是人之所知〔74〕

The cocks crow and the dogs bark—this is what we all know
and hear.

绝圣弃知，大盗乃止〔76〕

Discard the sages and wisdom, and the great robbers will be curbed...

君子不得已而临莅天下〔78〕

If the superior man has to rule over the world...

L

梁丽可以冲城而不可以窒穴〔80〕

A battering-ram can be used to knock down a city-wall but cannot be used to fill a hole...

M

明白于天地之德者〔82〕

A clear understanding of the virtue of the Heaven and the Earth is called...

P

庖丁为文惠君解牛〔84〕

A butcher was carving a bullock for Lord Wenhui.

庖人虽不治疱（越俎代庖）〔86〕

Even the cook is not attending to his duties...

Q

其动也天，其静也地〔88〕

He moves like a heavenly body and he is still like the Earth itself.

其所美者为神奇〔90〕

Beauty can be considered as something miraculous. . .

巧者劳而知者忧〔92〕

Those with adroit hands tire themselves physically. . .

且夫水之积也不厚（芥为之舟）〔94〕

If a mass of water is not deep enough, it will not be able to
float large ships.

穷则反，终则始〔96〕

Things turn to their opposites when they reach the limit, and
begin again when they reach the end.

丘山积卑而为高〔98〕

Hills and mountains become high when their low parts are
accumulated in them. . .

去小知而大知明〔100〕

Discard your petty wisdom and great wisdom will come into
being. . .

泉涸，鱼相与处于陆（相濡以沫）〔102〕
When a spring dries up, the fish are stranded on the land...

R

人大喜邪，毗于阳〔104〕
To be overjoyed is harmful to the yang element...

人莫鉴于流水而鉴于止水〔106〕
Men do not use running water as a mirror; they only use the still water.

人生天地之间，若白驹之过郤〔108〕
The life of a man between Heaven and Earth is as brief as the passage of a horse through a crevice in the wall.

人主莫不欲其臣之忠〔110〕
No monarch does not hope that his ministers will be loyal to him, but loyal ministers are not always trusted.

汝不知夫螳螂乎（螳臂挡车）〔112〕
(Qu Boyu said to Yan He) Don't you know the fable of the mantis?

S

上诚好知而无道〔114〕
When the rulers desire knowledge and neglect Tao...

圣人之用兵也〔116〕

When a sage wages a war, he can destroy a state without losing the support of the people.

施于人而不忘〔118〕

Doing a favor for people with the intention of receiving rewards is not a favor at all.

势为天子而不以贵骄人〔120〕

Some people may be as high and noble as kings, but they will not despise others because of their positions.

势为天子, 未必贵也〔122〕

A powerful emperor may not be high and noble...

水静则明烛须眉〔124〕

Peaceful waters have a clear and level surface that gives an image...

水流乎无形〔126〕

A stream of water runs without a fixed course from nowhere...

死生, 命也, 其有夜旦之常〔128〕

Life and death are destined, just like the eternal succession....

T

天地者, 万物之父母也〔130〕

The Heaven and the Earth give birth to all the things in the
world.

天道运而无所积，故万物成〔132〕
The natural course of events moves on and on so that everything
in the world comes into existence...

天与地无穷，人死者有时〔134〕
The Heaven and the Earth are limitless whereas the human
life is limited.

天下有道，则与物皆昌〔136〕
When the world is prevalent with Tao, he shares the prosperity
with everything...

W

万物殊理，道不私〔138〕
Each of all the things in the world has its own laws, but because
Tao does not show partiality to any of them...

万物职职，皆从无为殖〔140〕
There are so many things in the world. Everything in the
world is born with nothing having done anything.

为善无近名，为恶无近刑〔142〕
When you do good, don't do it for the sake of fame...

闻在宥天下，不闻治天下也〔144〕

I have heard of letting the world be and letting the world alone,
but I have never heard of governing the world.

无为为之之谓天〔146〕

To act by doing nothing is called the way of the Heaven...

无知无能者〔148〕

No one can avoid what he does not know and what is beyond
his power.

吾生也有涯，而知也无涯〔150〕

Man's life is limited but knowledge is unlimited.

X

昔者庄周梦为胡蝶〔152〕

I, by the name of Zhuang Zhou, once dreamed that I was a
butterfly...

西施病心而矉其里〔154〕

The famous beauty Xi Shi frowned at neighbors when she
had a heartache.

小惑易方，大惑易性〔156〕

A man with a mild confusion may change his direction of life;
a man with a serious confusion may change his inborn nature.

鱼处水而生，人处水而死〔174〕

Fish can only survive in waters while men will die in waters.

鱼相造乎水，人相造乎道〔176〕

As fish strive for water, so men strive for Tao.

Z

朝菌不知晦朔〔178〕

The fungi that sprout in the morning and die before evening
do not know the alternation of night and day...

知道易，勿言难〔180〕

It is not hard to understand Tao, but it is hard not to talk about it.

知其愚者，非大愚也〔182〕

If they are aware that they are foolish, they are not yet the
worst fools...

知士无思虑之变则不乐〔184〕

A man good at employing his wits is not happy when he does
not see the chances to develop his thoughts...

知天乐者，其生也天行〔186〕

He who understands heavenly joy follows nature when he is alive...

知天之所为，知人之所为者〔188〕

To know what the Heaven can do and to know what man can
do—that is the ultimate human knowledge.

知足者，不以利自累也〔190〕
He who is content with what he has will not exhaust himself
for any high position and handsome pay...

直木先伐，甘井先竭〔192〕
A straight tree is the first to be cut down; and a sweet well is
the first to be drawn dry.

至乐活身，唯无为几存〔194〕
In refrainment of action we are closest to perfect happiness
and enjoyment of life.

褚小者不可以怀大〔196〕
A small bag cannot hold large things...

朱泙漫学屠龙（屠龙之技）〔198〕
Zhu Pingman spent a fortune in learning the skill of killing dragons
from Zhili Yi.

庄子与惠子游于濠梁之上〔200〕
Zhuang Zi travelled with Hui Zi over a bridge on the Hao River.

庄子说

庄子,姓庄名周,字子修。战国宋国人。师长桑公子,受号南华仙人(唐天宝元年受号为南华真人)。出身于破落的显贵家族,青少年时期曾受过相当高的文化教养,但长成后却经受着家破国亡的痛苦。

庄子曾为漆园吏。相传楚威王闻其贤,厚币以迎,许以为相,辞不就。并说:"吾将曳尾于涂中。"

庄子主张"逍遥","扶摇而上者九万里"快哉!"观鱼"、"梦蝶"乐哉!其名言曰:"无欲而天下足,无为而万物化。""无为而尊者,天道也;有为而累者,人道也。""与人和者,谓之人乐;与天和者,谓之天乐。""巧者劳而知者忧,无能者无所求,饱食而遨游,泛若不系之舟。"

Zhuang Zi's name was Zhuang Zhou, with the courtesy name Zixiu. He was a native of the State of Song in the Warring States Period. He studied from Sang Gongzi, and was given the alternative name Nanhua Xianren [immortal] (in the first year of Tianbao period in the Tang Dynasty, he was conferred the title Nanhua Zhenren

[true man]). Born into a declined noble family, Zhuang Zi received relatively high education as a teenager, but suffered when growing up with his state subjugated and family wrecked.

Zhuang Zi used to be a guard of the Lacquer Garden. Legend has it that when King Weiwang of Chu heard of his wisdom, he invited him with handsome reward and promised him the post of prime minister, Zhuang Zi declined. He said, "I would like to lead a free and easy life like a tortoise waving his tail in mud."

Zhuang Zi favored "wandering in absolute freedom," "soaring to a height of 90,000 li," and "watching fish" and "dreaming being a butterfly." His famous sayings include: "The kings enriched the world by having no desires, and invigorated everything by doing nothing." "To do nothing and yet command respect is the natural way of Tao, while to do things and receive the trouble is the human way of Tao." "To be in harmony with men is called human joy. To be in harmony with nature is called heavenly joy." "Those with adroit hands tire themselves physically; those with wisdom tire themselves mentally. An incompetent person pursues nothing. With the stomach filled, he drifts, like a small boat without a cable. Such is the man who wanders freely."

安危相易，祸福相生

Safety and danger alternate with each other; good fortune and misfortune interchange with each other.

庄子说

安危相易，祸福相生，缓急相摩，聚散以成。此名实之可纪，精微之可志也。

《庄子·则阳》

Safety and danger alternate with each other; good fortune and misfortune interchange with each other; tense times and relaxed times succeed each other; collection and dispersion are related to each other. These names and realities can be recorded, and their particulars can be verified.

【注释】

易：变换，转化。祸福：见《老子》："祸兮，福之所倚；福兮，祸之所伏。"相摩：互相转化，互相影响。聚散以成：聚和散是相对而形成的，有聚才有散，有散才有聚。此：指以上各种现象。纪：记。志：记。

庄子认为道不仅是抽象的、同一的，同时又反映在万物的各种具体变化、对立的现象之中。

【译文】

安危互相转化，祸福相依相生，缓急互相变化，聚散相因而成。这就是名实可为纲纪，精微可以记述。

百年之木，破为牺尊

A hundred-year-old tree is sawed to make into a sacrificial vessel.

百年之木，破为牺尊，青黄而文之，其断在沟中。比牺尊于沟中之断，则美恶有间矣，其于失性一也。

《庄子·天地》

A hundred-year-old tree is sawed to make into a sacrificial vessel painted in blue and yellow patterns while the stump is left in the ditch. If we compare the sacrificial vessel with the stump in the ditch, one is appreciated and the other is neglected, but one thing is the same: both of them have lost their inborn nature.

【注释】

牺尊：雕刻成牺牛图形的尊，是名贵的祭神器具。**文**：粉饰，画上文彩。**其断在沟中**：大树被破断之后，没用的另一段丢弃在山沟里。**比牺尊于沟中之断**：把雕刻成牺尊与被丢弃在山沟里另一段相比。**间**：分别，差别。**失性**：丧失了树木本来的天性。**一**：相同。

【译文】

百年大树，砍伐破开雕制成祭神用的牺尊，涂上五颜六色的文彩，将剩下的废料丢弃在山沟里。如果将牺尊和被丢弃在山沟里的断木相比则有美和丑的差别，但在丧失了树木本来的天性这一点上两者却是相同的。

北冥有鱼，其名为鲲

In the North Sea there is a kind of fish by the name of kun.

庄子说

北冥有鱼，其名为鲲。鲲之大，不知其几千里也。化而为鸟，其名为鹏。鹏之背，不知其几千里也。怒而飞，其翼若垂天之云。

《庄子·逍遥游》

In the North Sea there is a kind of fish by the name of kun, whose size covers thousands of li. The fish metamorphoses into a kind of bird by the name of peng, whose back covers thousands of li. When it rises in flight, its wings are like clouds that hang from the sky.

【注释】

北冥：北海。冥（míng），同溟，指海。因海水深黑而又称"冥海"。鲲（kūn）：大鱼。鹏：传说中的神鸟。怒：奋飞的样子。垂天：天边。垂，通陲，边际。

【译文】

北海里有鱼，名字叫鲲。巨大无比，不知有几千里长。鲲变化为鸟，名字叫鹏，它的背不知有几千里长。大鹏奋起而飞，翅膀就像垂在天边的云彩。

彼窃钩者诛，窃国者为诸侯

Those who steal the knives are executed while those who usurp the states become princes.

彼窃钩者诛，窃国者为诸侯，诸侯之门而仁义存焉，则是非窃仁义圣知邪？

《庄子·胠箧》

Those who steal the knives are executed while those who usurp the states become princes. Now that benevolence and virtue are observed in the houses of the princes, does it not mean that benevolence, virtue and sagely wisdom have all been stolen?

【注释】

钩：铸金作钩形，像后世银锞之类。还有一种解释是衣带钩，代指不值钱的东西。圣：聪明。《老子》："绝圣弃智，民利百倍。"王弼注："圣，才之善也。"

【译文】

那些偷窃带钩的小偷被处死刑，而窃国大盗却成了诸侯，这些诸侯表面上还打着仁义的旗号，这难道不是盗窃了仁义圣智吗？

伯夷死名于首阳之下

Bo Yi died for his reputation on Mount Shouyang.

伯夷死名于首阳之下，盗跖死利于东陵之上。二人者，所死不同，其于残生伤性均也。奚必伯夷之是而盗跖之非也。

《庄子·骈拇》

Bo Yi died for his reputation on Mount Shouyang; Zhi the Robber died for wealth on Mount Dongling. These two people died for different reasons, but the damage done to their lives and the harm done to their inborn nature was one and the same. Why must we praise Bo Yi and denounce Zhi the Robber?

【注释】

伯夷：商孤竹君之长子。相传其父遗命要立次子叔齐为储君。孤竹君死后，叔齐让位伯夷，伯夷不受，叔齐亦不登位，兄弟二人先后逃到周国，因反对周武王伐纣，不食周粟逃到首阳山，采薇而食，最后饿死山中。死名：死于名，为名声而死。盗跖（zhí）：春秋时大盗。死利：为财利而死。东陵：山东章武有东陵山，传说山上有跖冢。

【译文】

伯夷为名节死在首阳山下，盗跖为财利死在东陵山上。这两个人死因虽不同，但在残生伤性这一点上却是一样的。既然如此，那又何必赞颂伯夷而非议盗跖呢！

不利货财，不近贵富

He will not crave for property and wealth and will not strive for fame and position.

老人家说系列丛书

庄子说

不利货财，不近贵富；不乐寿，
不哀夭；不荣通，不丑穷。

《庄子·天地》

He will not crave for property and wealth and will not strive for fame and position. He will not rejoice over longevity and will not grieve over premature death. He will not feel proud of being a high official and will not feel ashamed for being poor.

【注释】

利：作动词用。不利货财即不以货财为利。近：就。不近，即不要。不乐寿：不因长寿而高兴。不哀夭：不因短命而悲伤。不荣通：不因飞黄腾达而感到荣耀。不丑穷：不因穷困潦倒而感到羞愧。

【译文】

不谋财货，不近富贵；不因长寿而高兴，不因短命而悲伤；不以通达为荣，不以穷困为耻。

不忘其所始，不求其所终

The true man in ancient times did not forget the origin of his life; he did not explore the final destiny of his life.

不忘其所始，不求其所终。受而喜之，忘而复之。是之谓不以心捐道，不以人助天，是之谓真人。

《庄子·大宗师》

The true man in ancient times did not forget the origin of his life; he did not explore the final destiny of his life. He was pleased to accept whatever came to his life; he gave no thought to life and death as if he had returned to nature. This is what meant by not impairing Tao with the mind and not assisting the Heaven with human efforts. This is what the true man was like.

【注释】

始：生。终：死。受：得到。指得到天道所赋予的生命。忘：失。指生命的亡失。复之：复归于天道。

【译文】

（古代真人）不忘记自己的来源，不追求自己的归宿。获得生命欣然接受，失去生命则复归自然。这叫做不用心智去损害道，不用人为去帮助天，这就叫做真人。

蝉方得美荫而忘其身

A cicada had just found a fine spot in the shade and ignored the imminent danger.

蝉方得美荫而忘其身。螳螂执翳而搏之，见得而忘其形；异鹊从而利之，见利而忘其真。

《庄子·山木》

A cicada had just found a fine spot in the shade and ignored the imminent danger. A mantis hid itself behind the leaves snatching the cicada and ignoring the imminent danger. The extraordinary magpie in its turn took advantage of this situation and caught the mantis, entirely forgetting about its own disadvantage.

【注释】

忘其身：不注意自身的危险。执翳（yì）：举臂。螳螂臂前有锯齿，形状似翳（边上有锯齿形的旗）故称执翳。从而利之：从中取利，指食螳螂。真：本性。异鹊（大喜鹊）翼大可飞而不飞，眼大应见而不见，故说"忘其真"。看不见正有人拿弹弓瞄准了它。

【译文】

蝉得到一片好树荫而忘记自身的危险；藏在它身后的螳螂举臂抓住了它，螳螂有所得而忘记了自己所处的险境；异鹊从中取利抓住了螳螂，异鹊贪利也忘记了自己的性命之忧（看不见正有人拿弹弓瞄准了它）。

长者不为有余，短者不为不足

The long is not to be considered too much and the short is not to be considered too little.

长者不为有余，短者不为不足。
是故凫胫虽短，续之则忧；鹤胫虽长，
断之则悲。故性长非所断，性短非所
续，无所去忧也。

《庄子·骈拇》

The long is not to be considered too much and the short is not to be considered too little. Thus, short as the legs are, the duck will come to trouble if we stretch them out. Long as the legs are, the crane will come into grief if we cut them short. Therefore, something that is long by nature is not to be shortened; something that is short by nature is not to be lengthened. In this way, there will be no worry or care.

【注释】

凫（fú）：野鸭。胫：腿，脚。无所去忧：没有什么忧愁，所以无须抛弃什么。去，抛弃。

【译文】

长的并非多余，短的并非不足。所以，野鸭腿虽然短，人为接长只会造成它的痛苦；鹤的腿虽然长，人为截短就会造成它的悲哀。因而原本长的不能截短，原来短的也不能接长，这没有什么可以忧虑的。

唇竭则齿寒

Since the lips are gone, the teeth get cold.

唇竭则齿寒，鲁酒薄而邯郸围，圣人生而大盗起。

《庄子·胠箧》

Since the lips are gone, the teeth get cold; since the gift wine from the State of Lu was thin, the city of Handan (capital of the State of Zhao) got besieged; since the sages are born, the robbers appear in this world.

【注释】

竭：亡。成语"唇亡齿寒"出于此。意思是嘴唇没有了，牙齿就会受冻，比喻彼此利害关系十分密切（多指两个相邻的国家）。**鲁酒薄而邯郸围**：楚宣公朝会各国诸侯，鲁恭公迟到，而且献来的酒味淡。于是楚国出兵讨伐鲁国。梁惠王早有攻赵的想法，但一向怕楚国援助赵国，故乘楚讨伐鲁国的机会出兵攻打赵国，包围了赵国的都城邯郸。**生、起**：都是出现的意思。

【译文】

唇亡而齿寒，鲁国酒淡而殃及到赵国的都城邯郸遭围困，圣人出现而大盗兴起。

大声不入于里耳

Grand music will not appeal to the villagers.

大声不入于里耳，折杨、皇荂，则嗑然而笑。是故高言不止于众人之心，至言不出，俗言胜也。

《庄子·天地》

Grand music will not appeal to the villagers, but popular music will set them laughing heartily. Therefore, lofty speech will not remain in the hearts of the common people, great truth will not be spoken by the common people, and only worldly sayings are prevalent.

【注释】

大声：高雅的音乐，比喻作者的高论。里耳：俗里陋巷人的耳朵，代指孤陋寡闻的人。折扬、皇荂（huā）：通俗乐曲名。嗑（kè）：笑的状声词。高言：高论，指作者的理论。至言：即高言，至道之言。

【译文】

高雅的音乐不被俗里陋巷之人所欣赏，对一些（折杨、皇荂之类）俗曲则津津乐道。所以高明言论难于为众人所接受，至道之言隐而不显，流言俗语却泛滥于世。

道不可闻，闻而非也

As Tao cannot be heard, what can be heard is not Tao.

道不可闻，闻而非也；道不可见，见而非也；道不可言，言而非也。知形形之不形乎，道不当名。

《庄子·知北游》

As Tao cannot be heard, what can be heard is not Tao. As Tao cannot be seen, what can be seen is not Tao. As Tao cannot be spoken of, what can be spoken of is not Tao. Do you know that what creates the form is formless? Tao should not be given a name.

【注释】

形形之不形：支配有形的东西是无形的。道不当名：道是无形的，不该安他一个名称。《老子》："吾不知其名，字之曰道，强为之名曰大。"

庄子认为既然道是虚无的，因而不能听，不能见，不能说。

【译文】

道不可以听，听到的就不是道；道不可以看，看见的就不是道；道不可以说，说出来的就不是道。知道主宰有形的物是无形的道吧！道是无形的，不该给它安个名称。

道行之而成，物谓之而然

A path is formed because we walk on it; a thing has a name because we call it so.

道行之而成，物谓之而然。

《庄子·齐物论》

A path is formed because we walk on it; a thing has a name because we call it so.

【注释】

道：道路。物：万物。

在先秦理论界对名和实关系的争论中名辩派公孙龙提出"指非指"、"白马非马"的命题影响很大。而庄子认为这些争论都是一管之见，片面之辞。他认为对的就是对的，不对的就是不对的。路是人走出来的，事物的名称是人叫出来的，天下万物本来如此而已。

【译文】

道路是人走出来的，事物的名称是人叫出来的。

德有所长，而形有所忘

For men with ample virtue, their physical defects might be forgotten.

德有所长，而形有所忘。人不忘
其所忘，而忘其所不忘，此谓诚忘。

《庄子·德充符》

For men with ample virtue, their physical defects might
be forgotten. If people do not forget what they ought to forget
and forget what they ought not to forget, this is true forgetful-
ness.

【注释】

长（cháng）：善。忘：指对形体上的缺陷。**不忘其所忘**：即不忘其所应当忘记
的（指形体缺陷）。**忘其所不忘**：即忘其所不应当忘记的（指道德上的不足）。

【译文】

只要有过人的德性，形体上的缺陷就会被忘记。人
们如果不忘记所应当忘记的，而忘记所不应当忘记的，
那才是真正的忘记。

儿子终日嗥而嗌不嗄

A new-born baby can cry all day without losing its voice because it is in the perfection of equilibrium.

儿子终日嗥而嗌不嗄，和之至
也；终日握而手不掜，共其德也；终
日视而目不瞚，偏不在外也。

《庄子·庚桑楚》

A newborn baby can cry all day without losing its voice
because it is in the perfection of equilibrium. It can make
fists all day long without opening it because it is in the perfection of its nature. It can gaze all day without turning its
eyes because it is in the perfection of a concentrated mind.

【注释】

嗥（háo）：号叫。嗌（yì）：咽喉。嗄（shà）：通哑，沙哑。掜（niè）：拳曲。
共：合。瞚（shùn）：通瞬，眼睛转动。

庄子认为学道就要放弃得失，学婴儿那样天真无知，解除心理障碍，才能学道
有成。

【译文】

小孩子整天号哭而喉咙不哑，这是因为和气纯厚
（不是因为伤心而号哭）；整天握拳而手不曲，这是因为
这合乎自然的德性；整天注视某处而可以目不转睛，这
是因为他不偏注于所看的外物（目中无物）。

夫大壑之为物也

The vast sea is something you cannot fill by pouring in water and you cannot drain up by drawing water.

夫大壑之为物也，注焉而不满，酌焉而不竭。吾将游焉。

《庄子·天地》

The vast sea is something you cannot fill by pouring in water and you cannot drain up by drawing water. I'm going there for a trip.

【注释】

大壑：指东海，借指大道。**注**：灌。**酌**：取。**竭**：干涸。

作者将东海比喻为大道，故用游来比喻心神向往。

【译文】

作为大海，灌注而不会满溢，取之而不会干涸，我要去遨游一番。

夫富者，苦身疾作

Men of wealth toil and moil to accumulate more riches than they can possibly consume.

夫富者，苦身疾作，多积财而不得尽用，其为形也亦外矣。夫贵者，夜以继日，思虑善否，其为形也亦疏矣。

《庄子·至乐》

Men of wealth toil and moil to accumulate more riches than they can possibly consume. How superfluous they are in their way of valuing life! Men of distinction ponder over good and evil day and night. How irrelevant they are in their way of valuing life!

【注译】

苦身：使身体劳苦。**疾作：**拼命干活。**外：**相背离。**善否：**指官运亨通与阻滞。否（pǐ），本指《周易》中的卦名，意思是：天地不交而万物不通，故有阻塞、衰败的意思。**疏：**远。

【译文】

富有的人，劳苦身体，拼命经营，积聚了许多财物而不能充分享用，其实这样做与保养身体是相违背的。做官的人，一天到晚苦思暝想如何能够官运亨通，这样做与保养身体是相背离的。

夫鹄不日浴而白

The swans are white although they do not bathe themselves every day.

夫鹄不日浴而白，乌不日黔而黑。黑白之朴，不足以为辩。

《庄子·天运》

The swans are white although they do not bathe themselves every day; the crows are black although they do not dye themselves every day. As the intrinsic simplicity of black and white is not to be disputed over, so the extrinsic glory of fame and name is not to be exaggerated.

【注释】

鹄（hú）：天鹅。日浴：每天洗澡。乌：乌鸦。日黔：每日染黑。黔（qián），黑色，这里作动词用。黑白之朴：都是天然生成的颜色，故说朴。意即说万物各有各的本性，不能强行政变。辩：变。

【译文】

鹤不用天天洗澡也白，乌鸦不用天天染墨也黑。黑白都是天然生成的颜色，都不能强行使它改变。

夫水行不避蛟龙者，渔父之勇也

To travel by the water in defiance of the flood dragons shows the valour of the fishermen.

夫水行不避蛟龙者，渔父之勇也；陆行不避兕虎者，猎夫之勇也；白刃交于前，视死若生者，烈士之勇也；知穷之有命，知通之有时，临大难而不惧者，圣人之勇也。

《庄子·秋水》

To travel by the water in defiance of the flood dragons shows the valour of the fishermen; to travel on the land in defiance of the rhinos and tigers shows the valour of the hunters; to confront sword blades in defiance of death shows the valour of the warriors; to know that fortune and misfortune are determined by the times and to brave dangers without fear shows the valour of the sages.

【注释】

蛟：属龙而无角。渔父：渔夫。兕（sì）：雌性犀牛。

这是庄子借孔子对子路说的话，说明命运是由天道主宰的，穷通不能由人，在任何情况下都应该安时听命。

【译文】

入水中不避蛟龙，这是渔夫的勇敢；在陆地不避猛兽，这是猎人的勇敢；在刀光剑影中视死如归，这是烈士的勇敢；知道穷困是因为天命，通达是因为时势，面临大难而无所畏惧，这是圣人的勇敢。

夫天地至神，而有尊卑先后之序

If the Heaven and the Earth, which are the most sacred, have their distinction of rank and order.

夫天地至神，而有尊卑先后之序，而况人道乎！宗庙尚亲，朝廷尚尊，乡党尚齿，行事尚贤，大道之序也。

《庄子·天道》

If the Heaven and the Earth, which are the most sacred, have their distinction of rank and order, how much more so is the human way of life! Blood relations are honored in the ancestral temples; reverence is honored at court; seniority is honored in the neighborhood; worthiness is honored in the conduct of affairs—all this is the ordering in Tao.

【注释】

宗庙尚亲：宗族之内，是讲究亲疏的。尚，推崇，讲究。尊：指爵位的高低。齿：指年龄的大小。

【译文】

天地最为神明，尚有尊卑先后之序，何况人道！宗庙尚亲，朝庭尚尊，乡党之间推崇长者，任事推崇贤能，这是大道之序。

夫昭昭生于冥冥

Brightness originates from darkness.

夫昭昭生于冥冥，有伦生于无形，精神生于道，形本生于精，而万物以形相生。

《庄子·知北游》

Brightness originates from darkness, the visible from the invisible, the spirit from Tao, and the physical form from the energy of the spirit. All things are created with their respective forms and shapes.

【注释】

昭昭生于冥冥：意谓天地开辟，万物昭彰的景象是从昏昏暗暗、浑浑沌沌的远古时代演变来的。**伦**：纹理。有伦，有纹理结构，即有形。《天地》篇："物生成理谓之形。"**形本**：形体。**精**：精神。**万物以形相生**：万物以各种形态互相转化。

【译文】

光明产生于昏暗，有形产生于无形，精神产生于道，形体产生于精神，万物以各种形态互相转化。

狗不以善吠为良

As a dog is not considered good merely because it barks well.

狗不以善吠为良，人不以善言为贤。

《庄子·徐无鬼》

As a dog is not considered good merely because it barks well, so a man is not considered wise merely because he speaks well.

【注释】

善吠：吠，（狗）叫。

作者主张做人要无为、无言、无求，遵循天道。所以他借孔子的话说："生前不追求爵位，死后不求谥号，不聚敛钱财，不树立名声，这才是大人。"

【译文】

狗不因为会叫就是好狗，人不因为会说就是贤才。

古之所谓得志者，非轩冕之谓也

By "fulfillment of ambition," the men of ancient times did not mean obtaining high ranks of office.

古之所谓得志者，非轩冕之谓也，谓其无以益其乐而已矣。今之所谓得志者，轩冕之谓也。

《庄子·缮性》

By "fulfillment of ambition," the men of ancient times did not mean obtaining high ranks of office, but meant enjoying infinite pleasure. By "fulfillment of ambition," the men of today mean obtaining high ranks of office.

【注释】

轩冕：车子和衣冠，代指高官厚禄。无以益其乐：纯实之性无以复加。

作者认为：高官厚禄在身，并不是性命所固有的，而是如同外物偶然而来，寄托一时而已。寄托的东西，来时不能抵挡，去时不可挽留。所以不要为高官厚禄而恣纵心志，也不要因为穷困而趋炎附势，两者同样快乐，无须忧虑。

【译文】

古代所谓得志者，并不指得到了高官厚禄，而是指得到了无以复加的快乐。现在所说的得志者，就是指得到了高官厚禄。

古之畜天下者，无欲而天下足

In ruling over the world in ancient times, the kings enriched the world by having no desires.

古之畜天下者，无欲而天下足，无为而万物化，渊静而百姓定。

《庄子·天地》

In ruling over the world in ancient times, the kings enriched the world by having no desires, invigorated everything by doing nothing, and pacified the people by keeping quiet.

【注释】

畜：养育。历来的统治者都把自己说成是养育老百姓的。渊静：像深渊里的水一样平静。定：安定。

作者认为君主无为平静，百姓就可以安定了。

【译文】

古时候君主治理天下，君主无贪欲而天下富足，无为而万物自化，清静而百姓自然安定。

古之至人，先存诸己而后存诸人

The perfect men in the past saw to it that they had Tao in themselves before they passed it on to others.

古之至人，先存诸己而后存诸人。所存于己者未定，何暇至于暴人之所行！

《庄子·人间世》

The perfect men in the past saw to it that they had Tao in themselves before they passed it on to others. You haven't had it in yourself yet, how can you expect to care for the behaviors of a tyrant?

【注释】

先存诸己而后存诸人：先在自己身上确立起来（指道的修养），然后才能培养别人。存，立。诸，"之于"合音。未定：动摇不定。何暇至于暴人之所行：哪里谈得上能够感化暴人的所作所为。何暇，哪来得及。至于，及于。暴人，恶人。《墨子·尚同下》："善人赏而暴人罚，则国必治矣。"

【译文】

古代的圣人，先充实自己，然后再去扶持别人。如果自己都站不稳，还怎么去纠正恶人的行为呢？

官施而不失其宜

The sage places his officials in appropriate positions, and promotes his officials according to their talents.

官施而不失其宜，拔举而不失其能，毕见其情事而行其所为，行言自为而天下化。

《庄子·天地》

The sage places his officials in appropriate positions, and promotes his officials according to their talents. He makes thorough investigations before he takes action. His words and deeds affect the people naturally so that all the people are transformed.

【注释】

官施：设官施令。拔举：指选拔人才。毕见：看清。句谓看清事情的真相然后顺应形势而做所应该做的事。行言自为而天下化：一言一行都是圣人自然而然地发出的，那么天下的百姓就自然受到感化了。

【译文】

设官施令得当，选拔依据才能，明察真情而做所应该做的，任其自为而百姓自然从化。

观之名则不见，求之利则不得

He owns nothing in terms of possession and fame.

观之名则不见，求之利则不得，缭意绝体而争此，不亦惑乎！

《庄子·盗跖》

He owns nothing in terms of possession and fame. Isn't he senseless to exhaust the mind and fatigue the body to strive for fame and gain!

【注释】

观之名则不见：名声得不到。观，察。利则不得：利也得不到。缭意：心慌意乱，绝体：竭尽全力。

作者认为知足无争，保养心性，才是长生安乐之道。

【译文】

名和利都是身外的空虚之物，劳心伤体地去争这些东西，这不是糊涂吗！

何谓道？ 有天道，有人道

What do we mean by Tao? There is the Tao in the natural way and there is the Tao in the human way.

何谓道？有天道，有人道。无为而尊者，天道也；有为而累者，人道也。

《庄子·在宥》

What do we mean by Tao? There is the Tao in the natural way and there is the Tao in the human way. To do nothing and yet command respect is the natural way of Tao, while to do things and receive the trouble is the human way of Tao. The ruler should practice the natural way of Tao and the subjects should practice the human way of Tao.

【注释】

尊：尊贵。累：劳累。

说明天道与人道的关系。天道无为，人道有为；天道为主，人道为次；天道为上，人道为下。庄子强调的是天道，但又不完全抹杀人道。

【译文】

什么是道？道有天道，有人道。无为而尊贵的，是天道；有为而劳累的，是人道。

虎之与人异类，而媚养己者，顺也

The tiger is of a different species from man, yet it is gentle to its keeper because the keeper complies with its disposition.

虎之与人异类，而媚养己者，顺
也；故其杀者，逆也。

《庄子·人间世》

The tiger is of a different species from man, yet it is gentle to its keeper because the keeper complies with its disposition. The tiger gets murderous only when it is irritated.

【注释】

媚养己者：媚顺于饲养自己的人。媚，柔顺，温顺。**杀**：指伤人。**逆**：触犯。指人触犯了虎。虎性虽暴，顺之就可以媚人，逆之就可以伤人。作者以此比喻，说明对待君主有时"顺"着他是很重要的。

【译文】

老虎和人不属于同类，但它却对饲养它的人很温顺，这是因为养虎的人顺着它的性子的缘故；老虎伤人，是因为人触犯了它。

惠子谓庄子曰（无用之用）

Hui Zi said to Zhuang Zi, "Your words are useless."

惠子谓庄子曰："子言无用。"庄子曰："知无用而始可与言用矣。夫地非不广且大也，人之所用容足耳，然则厕足而垫之致黄泉，人尚有用乎？"

《庄子·外物》

Hui Zi said to Zhuang Zi, "Your words are useless." Zhuang Zi said, "You have to know what is useless before I can talk to you about what is useful. Although the Earth is vast and broad, you can only possess the tiny bit of it where you put your feet. If, however, you dig the earth around your feet until you reach the hell, will the tiny bit of the Earth where you put your feet be useful?"

【注释】

　　人之所用容足耳：人只是用可容立足的地方，其余的地方并没有用。**厕**（cè）：通侧。**垫**（diàn）：陷下，作动词，使之陷，犹下掘。**人尚有用乎**：除置足之地外均成深渊，必然胆战心惊而无法立足，所以连置足之地也变得无用了。

【译文】

　　惠子对庄子说："你的言论无用。"庄子说："知道了无用才可以和你谈论有用的问题。大地并非不广大，而人所用的只是容足之地罢了。然而如果把立足之外的地方都向下挖掘到黄泉，人所立足的这块小地方还有用吗？"

惠子相梁，庄子往见之

When Hui Zi became the prime minister in the State of Liang，Zhuang Zi was going to see him.

惠子相梁，庄子往见之。或谓惠子曰："庄子来，欲代子相。"于是惠子恐，搜于国中三日三夜。

《庄子·秋水》

When Hui Zi became the prime minister in the State of Liang, Zhuang Zi was going to see him. Someone said to Hui Zi, "Zhuang Zi is coming. He wished to replace you as the prime minister." Thereupon, Hui Zi grew afraid and sent people to search for Zhuang Zi for three days and nights.

【注释】

惠子：惠施，曾为梁惠王相。或：有人。恐：指怕庄子取代自己的相位。

庄子去见惠施，对他说："南方有一种鸟，名叫鹓鶵，你知道吗？鹓鶵从南海出发，飞往北海，沿途非梧桐树不栖息，不是竹实不吃，不是甘美的泉水不喝。这时猫头鹰抓到一只死老鼠，看见鹓鶵经过，仰头对它说：'吓！你不要抢我的死老鼠！'现在你难道也怕我会抢你的相位吗？"

【译文】

惠子在魏国为相，庄子去见他。有人对惠施说："庄子来，想取代您的相位。"惠施听了很害怕，下令在国内（都城内）搜捕庄子三天三夜。

祸福淳淳

Good fortune and bad fortune have their comings and goings.

祸福淳淳，至有所拂者而有所宜；自殉殊面；有所正者有所差，比于大宅，百材皆度。

《庄子·则阳》

Good fortune and bad fortune have their comings and goings, pros and cons. In their pursuit after different aims, the people may be right or may be wrong. When you look around a big house, you will see different timber of different sizes, for different purposes.

【注释】

淳淳：流行的样子。**至有所拂者而有所宜**：时世的变化，一方面是矛盾的，另一方面又是统一的。拂，逆乱，矛盾。宜，适合，统一。**自殉殊面**：各走各的路。殉，逐。面，向。**有所正者有所差**：从某方面说是正确的，但从另一方面说又是错误的。**比于大宅，百材皆度**：譬如建造大屋，各种材料各有各的用处，因而没有不符合尺寸的。比，比方。

【译文】

祸福的流行，一方面看是矛盾的，另一方面看又是统一的，各自向着自己的方向发展。既有正确的也有错误的，好比建造大屋，各种不同规格的材料各有各的用处，因而各有各的尺寸。

鉴明则尘垢不止

There is no dust on a bright mirror while a dusty mirror is not bright.

鉴明则尘垢不止，止则不明也。
久与贤人处则无过。

《庄子·德充符》

There is no dust on a bright mirror while a dusty mirror is not bright. If you stay with a sage for a long time, you will be free of faults.

【注释】

鉴明：鉴，镜子。明，光亮。镜子光亮，灰尘就不会沾染，沾染了灰尘镜子就不够光亮。这个比喻说明：人心纯洁，就没有龌龊的想法，有了龌龊的想法，就说明心地不够纯洁。

【译文】

镜子明亮就不落灰尘，落上灰尘就不明亮了。经常和贤人相处就没有过失。

今且有人于此（随侯之珠）

If a man is now shooting with a precious pearl at a sparrow flying high in the sky, he will surely be laughed at.

今且有人于此，以随侯之珠弹千
仞之雀，世必笑之。是何也？则其所
用者重而所要者轻也。

《庄子·让王》

If a man is now shooting with a precious pearl at a sparrow flying high in the sky, he will surely be laughed at. Why? Because he is paying such a high price for an insignificant gain.

【注释】

今且：假设之辞。随侯之珠：古代名珠，被随国国君所得，故名。要：取。

庄子认为为了富贵权位而危害身心是一种不明轻重，本末倒置的表现，无疑就是"以随侯之珠弹千仞之雀"者也。

【译文】

假如现在有一个人，用宝贵的随侯之珠当作弹子去射高空的飞鸟，大家肯定会笑话他。为什么呢？因为他用贵重的东西去求取轻贱之物。

金石有声，不考不鸣。

Though musical instruments may give sounds, they will not ring unless they are struck.

金石有声，不考不鸣。

《庄子·天地》

Though musical instruments may give sounds，they will
not ring unless they are struck.

【注释】

考：敲击。

庄子认为道幽深静寂，清澈澄明。钟磬如不得道，便无从鸣响。所以说钟磬虽
然会发声，不敲则不鸣。

【译文】

钟磬虽然可以发出声响，但不敲则不鸣。

井蛙不可以语于海者

You cannot discuss the sea with a frog at the bottom of a well.

井蛙不可以语于海者，拘于虚也；夏虫不可以语于冰者，笃于时矣；曲士不可以语于道者，束于教也。

《庄子·秋水》

You cannot discuss the sea with a frog at the bottom of a well because it is confined to its dwelling place; you cannot discuss ice with a summer moth because it is limited to one season; you cannot discuss Tao with a bookworm because he is restrained to the book knowledge.

【注释】

语于海：谈及大海。拘：局限。虚：同墟。指井蛙所生活的地方。语于冰：谈及冰。笃于时：受时间限制。夏虫生活在夏天，冬天结冰时已死，故说"笃于时"。笃（dǔ），守，限制。曲士：一曲之士，即孤陋寡闻的人。

【译文】

不可以和井底之蛙谈论大海，因为它局限于狭小的活动空间；不可以和夏天的虫子谈论冰雪，因为它受生存时间的限制；不可以和孤陋寡闻的人说道，因为他被所受教育的束缚。

鸡鸣狗吠是人之所知

The cocks crow and the dogs bark—this is what we all know and hear.

鸡鸣狗吠，是人之所知。虽有大知，不能以言读其所自化，又不能以意其所将为。

《庄子·则阳》

The cocks crow and the dogs bark—this is what we all know and hear. But the wisest of us cannot describe in words why the cocks crow and the dogs bark or imagine in our minds what they will do in future.

【注释】

读：称，表达。其所自化：指鸡鸣狗吠自然变化所包含的意思。以意其所将为：凭着它（指鸡鸣狗吠）来意测出鸡狗想要干的事情。以、凭。

【译文】

鸡鸣狗叫，这是人所常听到的。但即使最聪明的人也不能用语言说出它们为什么鸣叫，也无法根据叫声判断出它们想要干什么。

绝圣弃知，大盗乃止

Discard the sages and wisdom, and the great robbers will be curbed.

绝圣弃知，大盗乃止，擿玉毁珠，小盗不起；焚符破玺，而民朴鄙；掊斗折衡，而民不争；殚残天下之圣法，而民始可与论议。

《庄子·胠箧》

Discard the sages and wisdom, and the great robbers will be curbed; destroy the jades and pearls, and the petty robbers will not appear; break the tallies and seals, and the people will be unsophisticated; crush the weights and scales, and the people will no longer quarrel; abolish all the sagely laws, and the people will be able to listen to reason.

【注释】

绝圣弃知：绝、弃，都是抛弃的意思。擿（zhì）：同掷，扔掉。掊（pǒu）斗折衡：把斗和称之类打碎折断。殚（dān）残：彻底摧毁。

【译文】

抛弃圣智，大盗才能平息；毁弃珠玉，小偷才不会兴起；焚毁君主的印信，百姓就会变得纯朴；折毁斗衡，百姓就不会争利；彻底摧毁天下的圣智法度，才可以与老百姓谈论道。

君子不得已而临莅天下

If the superior man has to rule over the world...

君子不得已而临莅天下，莫若无为。无为也而后安其性命之情。

《庄子·在宥》

If the superior man has to rule over the world, the best thing he can do is to do nothing. Let the world be and then he can secure the inborn nature of the people.

【注释】

莅（h）：到。临莅天下，就天子之位。

庄子认为，如果不得已而要当天子，最好是无为而治，不要有心去统治天下，而任天下百姓之自然。人人心性安定，天下就自然太平。如果扰乱人心，天下就不可能长治久安。

【译文】

君子如果不得已而君临天下，最好是无为而治。无为才能安定性命之情。

梁丽可以冲城而不可以窒穴

A battering-ram can be used to knock down a city-wall but cannot be used to fill a hole.

梁丽可以冲城而不可以窒穴，言殊器也；骐骥骅骝一日而驰千里，捕鼠不如狸狌，言殊技也；鸱鸺夜撮蚤，察毫末，昼出瞋目而不见丘山，言殊性也。

《庄子·秋水》

A battering-ram can be used to knock down a city-wall but cannot be used to fill a hole, for the use of the implements are different. A good steed can gallop a thousand li a day but cannot equal a cat or a weasel in catching the mice, for the skills of the animals are different. An owl can catch fleas and see the tip of a hair at night but cannot see a hill with its eyes wide open at daytime, for the inborn natures of the birds are different.

【注释】

梁丽：梁栋，大木。殊器：指用场不同，所用器具也不同。器，器具。骐骥骅骝（huá liú）：都是骏马。狸狌：狸，野猫。狌，黄鼠狼。技：本领。鸱鸺（chū xiāo）：猫头鹰。撮：抓。蚤：跳蚤。瞋目：张大眼睛。

【译文】

梁栋可以用来撞毁城墙，但却不能用来堵塞小洞，这是说器具的用场不同；骏马一日可行千里，但是捕鼠却不如猫和黄鼠狼，这是说技能不同；猫头鹰在夜里可以捕捉跳蚤，明察秋毫，但在白天睁大眼睛连山丘也看不见，这是说物性不同。

明白于天地之德者

A clear understanding of the virtue of the Heaven
and the Earth is called. . .

　　明白于天地之德者，此之谓大本大宗，与天和者也。所以均调天下，与人和者也。与人和者，谓之人乐。与天和者，谓之天乐。

《庄子·天道》

　　A clear understanding of the virtue of the Heaven and the Earth is called "the most fundamental principle", which means "harmony with nature." To bring equality and accord to the world is to be in harmony with men. To be in harmony with men is called "human joy". To be in harmony with nature is called "heavenly joy".

【注释】

　　天地之德：即无为。大本大宗：最根本。天：自然。和：顺。均调天下：使天下均平调协。意谓无为是用来调和社会矛盾、调和人与人之间的矛盾的。

【译文】

　　明白无为而治就是知道了根本，与自然和顺，使天下均平调协。与人和睦，称为人乐，与天和顺，称为天乐。

庖丁为文惠君解牛

A butcher was carving a bullock for Lord Wenhui.

庖丁为文惠君解牛，手之所触，肩之所倚，足之所履，膝之所踦，砉然响然，奏刀騞然，莫不中音，合于桑林之舞，乃中经首之会。

《庄子·养生主》

A butcher was carving a bullock for Lord Wenhui. At every touch of his hand, every move of his shoulder, every stamp of his foot and every nudge of his knee, there came the sound of slicing the flesh and wielding the knife—a perfect rhythm to the Dance of Mulberry Trees and a perfect tune of the music in King Yao's time.

【注释】

庖（páo）丁：厨工。文惠君：梁惠王。解牛：宰牛。解，分解，宰。踦（yǐ）：通倚，抵住。砉（huà）然：形容解牛时皮骨肉分离的声音。奏刀：进刀。騞（huō）：状声词。中（zhòng）音：合于乐音。

【译文】

庖丁为梁惠王宰牛，只见他手抓肩扛，脚踩膝抵，井然有序，不急不慢，进刀割解，霍霍有声，动作就像《桑林》舞的动作一样轻松悠然，那声音就像《经首》乐章中音符一样合谐动听。

庖人虽不治庖 （越俎代疱）

Even the cook is not attending to his duties.

庖人虽不治庖，尸祝不越樽俎而代之矣。

《庄子·逍遥游》

Even the cook is not attending to his duties, the priest at the offering ceremony will not come to the kitchen to do it for him.

【注释】

庖（páo）人：厨师。治庖：治理厨房的工作，如煮烹之类。尸祝：主持祭祀的人。樽（zūn）：古代酒器。俎（zǔ）：古代祭祀时盛放牛羊祭品的礼器。成语"越俎代庖"源于此。意思是厨师虽不在厨房做饭，司祭也不能放下祭品去替他下厨房。后以"越俎代庖"比喻超越自己职责范围去处理别人所管的事。

【译文】

厨师虽不下厨，但司祭也不会替他下厨做饭的。

其动也天，其静也地

He moves like a heavenly body and he is still like the Earth itself.

其动也天，其静也地，一心定而王天下；其鬼不崇，其魂不疲，一心定而万物服。

《庄子·天道》

He moves like a heavenly body and he is still like the Earth itself. When his mind is settled down, he will get to rule over the whole world. His physical form does not suffer from illness and his spirit will not get weary. When his mind is settled down, everything in the world will submit to him.

【注释】

其动也天，其静也地：动如天一样动，静如地一样静。即动静都是自然而然的。**一心定**：专心于静寂的境界。**崇（suì）**：鬼神给人造成灾祸。**魂**：精神。

【译文】

动则如天运转，静则如地寂然，专心于寂静的境界则统治天下；其鬼不为害，精神不疲劳，专心于静寂的境界而万物归服。

其所美者为神奇

Beauty can be considered as something miraculous.

其所美者为神奇，其所恶者为臭腐，臭腐复化为神奇，神奇复化为臭腐。

《庄子·知北游》

Beauty can be considered as something miraculous while ugliness can be considered obnoxious. Something obnoxious can be transformed into something miraculous and something miraculous can be transformed into something obnoxious.

【注释】

其所美者为神奇，其所恶者为臭腐：意谓神奇与臭腐都只不过是人们根据自己的好恶而定的，并没有什么固定的标准。**臭腐复化为神奇，神奇复化为臭腐：**两者随人的好恶而互相转化，循环不止。我们常说"化腐朽为神奇"出于此。

【译文】

觉得美的便视之为神奇，丑的便视之为腐朽；腐朽可以转化为神奇，神奇也可以转化为腐朽。

巧者劳而知者忧

Those with adroit hands tire themselves physically.

巧者劳而知者忧，无能者无所求，饱食而遨游，泛若不系之舟，虚而遨游者也？

《庄子·列御寇》

Those with adroit hands tire themselves physically; those with wisdom tire themselves mentally. An incompetent person pursues nothing. With the stomach filled, he drifts, like a small boat without a cable. Such is the man who wanders freely.

【注释】

无能者：即无为者，指得道者。**泛：**飘浮不定的样子。**虚而遨游者也：**虚则心无症结，无所共鸣，无劳无忧，故能逍遥游。

作者认为做到虚无宁静，安于所安，生无为，死无葬，任其自然，才是真正懂得大道。

【译文】

智巧的人忧劳，无为的人无所求，饱食而遨游，飘浮不定就像一叶不羁的小船，空虚心志而逍遥游。

且夫水之积也不厚（芥为之舟）

If a mass of water is not deep enough, it will not be able to float large ships.

　　且夫水之积也不厚，则其负大舟也无力。覆杯水于坳堂之上，则芥为之舟。置杯焉则胶，水浅而舟大也。

《庄子·逍遥游》

　　If a mass of water is not deep enough, it will not be able to float large ships. When you pour a cup of water into a hole on the ground of the courtyard, a straw can sail on it as a boat, but a cup will get stuck in it for the water is too shallow and the vessel is too large.

【注释】

　　且夫：表示要进一步论述，有提起下文的作用。且，连词。夫，助词。**负**：承载。**覆**：倒。**坳（ào）堂**：堂中低洼处。**芥为之舟**：那就只有小草可以当船。芥，小草。**胶**：粘住，沉下去。

【译文】

　　水积得不深，就承载不起大船。在堂前洼地上倒一杯水，小草就可以当船。如果放上一只杯子，就粘住了，这是因为水浅而"船"大的原因。

穷则反，终则始

Things turn to their opposites when they reach the limit, and begin again when they reach the end.

穷则反，终则始，此物之所有。

《庄子·则阳》

Things turn to their opposites when they reach the limit, and begin again when they reach the end. These are the universal laws of all the things in the world.

【注释】

穷则反：物极必反。穷，极。所有：所具有的现象。

庄子认为安危互相变换，祸福相伴相生，缓急互相转化，聚散相因而成。这就是名实可为纲纪，精微可以记述。所以，认识道的人，不追寻物的终结，不探求物的起源。

【译文】

物极必反，终则复始，这是万物所具有的现象。

丘山积卑而为高

Hills and mountains become high when their low parts are accumulated in them.

丘山积卑而为高，江河合水而为大，大人合并而为公。

《庄子·则阳》

Hills and mountains become high when their low parts are accumulated in them; the Yangtze River and the Yellow River become large when rivulets and streams flow into them; men endowed with Tao become humane when all the individual traits are manifested in them.

【注释】

大人：得道之人，合并：指容合众人。

【译文】

丘山聚积卑小而高，江河汇合众流而大，得道之人容合众人而大公无私。

去小知而大知明

Discard your petty wisdom and great wisdom will come into being.

去小知而大知明，去善而自善
矣。婴儿生无硕师而能言，与能言者
处也。

《庄子·外物》

Discard your petty wisdom and great wisdom will come
into being; discard your pretentious goodness and natural
goodness will come into being. The baby learns to speak
without learned teachers because it lives among people who
can speak.

【注释】

小知：指常人狭隘的智慧。**大知**：指得道者的智慧，以无智为智。**去善而自善**：抛弃常人所追求的小善就自然得天道的大善，以不善为善。**硕师**：大师。硕，原文作"石"，依唐写本改。**与能言者处也**：说明随俗自然就行了。处，共同生活。

庄子认为应该抛弃聪明智慧，随俗自然，才是大智。

【译文】

去除小智则大智才明，去掉小善则大善自显。婴儿生来没有老师教就会说话，这是因为与会说话的人生活在一起的缘故。

泉涸，鱼相与处于陆（相濡以沫）

When a spring dries up, the fish are stranded on the land.

泉涸，鱼相与处于陆，相呴以湿，相濡以沫，不如相忘于江湖。

《庄子·大宗师》

When a spring dries up, the fish are stranded on the land, moistening each other with their breath and dampening each other with their slime. But it would be much better for them to live in the rivers and lakes and forget each other.

【注释】

涸（hé）：水干。**相呴以湿**：用湿气互相呼吸。呴（xū），吐气。**相濡以沫**：用口沫来互相沾湿。濡（rú），湿润。**相忘**：相互忘掉。

成语"相濡以沫"、"濡沫涸辙"、"相呴相濡"皆出于此。意谓处于困境之中，互相竭力救助。

【译文】

泉水干涸，鱼儿困在陆地上互相吐口水以沾湿求生，倒不如在江湖里互不认识而自由自在的生活。

人大喜邪，毗于阳

To be overjoyed is harmful to the yang element.

　　人大喜邪，毗于阳；大怒邪，毗于阴。阴阳并毗，四时不至，寒暑之和不成，其反伤人之形乎！

《庄子·在宥》

　　To be overjoyed is harmful to the yang element, while to be exasperated is harmful to the yin element. When both yin and yang are in disorder, people will be unable to adapt themselves to the four seasons or to acclimatize themselves to hot and cold. As a result, they will suffer physically for it.

【注释】

　　毗（pí）：伤，偏。阴阳：阴阳调和，人的身体才能安康。偏于阳就表现为阴虚或阴亏病症；偏于阴就表现为阳虚或阳亏病症。阴阳并毗，就成了阴阳俱虚。大喜、大怒都会影响人的身体健康。

【译文】

　　人过分欢乐，就会伤害阳气；过分忧愤，就会伤害阴气。阴阳并伤，则四时不顺，寒暑不和，这样岂不是伤害了人的身体。

人莫鉴于流水而鉴于止水

Men do not use running water as a mirror; they only use the still water.

人莫鉴于流水而鉴于止水。唯止能止众止。

《庄子·德充符》

Men do not use running water as a mirror; they only use the still water. Only things that are still in themselves can still other things.

【注释】

莫：没有。鉴：照。止水：静止的水。唯止能止众止：只有静止的水才能使大家停下来临照。

这是作者借孔子的话，以静止的水喻静寂无为。

【译文】

没有人在流水上照自己的形象，而都是在静止的水面上去照。可见，只有静止的东西才能使大家静止。

人生天地之间，若白驹之过郤

The life of a man between Heaven and Earth is as brief as the passage of a horse through a crevice in the wall.

人生天地之间，若白驹之过郤，忽然而已。

《庄子·知北游》

The life of a man between Heaven and Earth is as brief as the passage of a horse through a crevice in the wall.

【注释】

白驹过郤：白驹，骏马，喻指日影。郤，通隙，缝隙，空隙。陆德明释文："郤，本亦作隙。隙，孔也。"意谓像白色的骏马在缝隙前飞快地越过，比喻时间过得极快。成语"白驹过隙"出于此。

这是庄子借老子对孔子说的话，认为人的生死只是"道"一瞬间的变化。

【译文】

人生活在天地之间，就像骏马在缝隙前飞快地越过，一闪而已。

人主莫不欲其臣之忠

No monarch does not hope that his ministers will be loyal to him, but loyal ministers are not always trusted.

庄子说

人主莫不欲其臣之忠，而忠未必信，故伍员流于江，苌弘死于蜀……人亲莫不欲其子之孝，而孝未必爱，故孝己忧而曾参悲。

《庄子·外物》

No monarch does not hope that his ministers will be loyal to him, but loyal ministers are not always trusted. Therefore, Wu Zixu was killed and thrown into the Yangtze River and Chang Hong was killed in Shu... No parent does not hope that his children will be filial to him, but filial sons are not always loved. Therefore, Xiao Ji was grieved and Zeng Can was sorrowful.

【注释】

伍员：原楚国人，后投奔吴王夫差。**苌弘**（chǎng hóng）：周敬王时大夫，晋赵鞅伐周，周人杀苌弘于蜀。**爱**：指得到父母的爱。**孝己**：殷高宗的儿子，遭后母虐待，苦闷而死。**曾参**：对父母十分孝顺，但常常被父母毒打，所以经常悲泣。

【译文】

君主都希望臣下对自己忠心耿耿，但忠心未必就被信任，所以伍员浮尸于江，苌弘死在蜀地……父母都希望儿子孝顺，但孝顺未必就能为父母所爱，所以孝己忧闷而死，曾参常常悲泣。

汝不知夫螳螂乎（螳臂挡车）

(Qu Boyu said to Yan He) Don't you know the fable of the mantis?

汝不知夫螳螂乎！怒其臂以当车辙，不知其不胜任也。是其才之美者也。

《庄子·人间世》

(Qu Boyu said to Yan He) Don't you know the fable of the mantis? The mantis raises its forelegs to stop the wheel of an oncoming chariot, unaware that this is beyond its power. This is because it is too assured of itself.

【注释】

怒：奋举。当：通挡。辙：本指车轮碾过的痕迹。此指车轮。是：作动词，有特的意思。美：得意的意思。这是庄子借蘧伯玉对颜阖说的话。

【译文】

(蘧伯玉对颜阖说) 你不知道螳螂吗！它奋力举起臂膀去阻挡车轮，却不知道自己的力量不能胜任，这是因为它过高地估计了自己的本事。

上诚好知而无道

When the rulers desire knowledge and neglect Tao...

上诚好知而无道，则天下大乱矣。

《庄子·胠箧》

When the rulers desire knowledge and neglect Tao, the world comes into great chaos.

【注释】

庄子主张执政者要清静无为，他认为远古时代人民结绳记事，都感到饮食可口，服饰华美，习俗快乐，居所安逸，邻国之间相望，鸡鸣犬吠的声音可以互相听到，人们一生却不相往来。那样的社会才是最好的社会。而现在（当时）的社会，人们为了崇尚贤才，内弃家人，外弃为主人所干的工作，足迹遍及列国，他认为这都是执政者推崇才智的过错。所以他主张"绝圣弃知"。

【译文】

执政者推崇才智而无道，天下就要大乱。

圣人之用兵也

When a sage wages a war, he can destroy a state without losing the support of the people.

圣人之用兵也，亡国而不失人心，利泽施于万物，不为爱人。

《庄子·大宗师》

When a sage wages a war, he can destroy a state without losing the support of the people. He can bestow favors on all the things in the world without being himself a true lover of the people.

【注释】

亡国而不失人心：圣人能顺从人心而用兵，故亡国也能不失人心。不为爱人：不是出于有意爱人之心。

【译文】

圣人用兵，灭亡了故国而不失掉民心，恩泽施及万物，并非出于有意爱人之心。

施于人而不忘

Doing a favor for people with the intention of receiving rewards is not a favor at all.

施于人而不忘，非天布也，商贾不齿。

《庄子·列御寇》

Doing a favor for people with the intention of receiving rewards is not a favor at all. Even merchants hold such conducts in contempt.

【注释】

施于人：施恩惠于人。不忘：总是以恩人自居。天布：出于自然的布施。商贾（gǔ）不齿：商人做买卖为了获利，而"施于人而不忘"的人，也是为了收买名利，而又装着施恩于人的样子，故连商贾都不如。

【译文】

施恩惠于人而念念不忘，这不是自然的布施，连商贾都看不起这样的人。

势为天子而不以贵骄人

Some people may be as high and noble as kings, but they will not despise others because of their positions.

势为天子而不以贵骄人，富有天下而不以财戏人。

《庄子·盗跖》

Some people may be as high and noble as kings, but they will not despise others because of their positions. Some people may possess as much as the world, but they will not be domineering because of their wealth.

【注释】

戏人：戏弄、侮辱人。

作者认为"势为天子，未必贵也；穷为匹夫，未必贱也。贵贱之分，在行之美恶。"

【译文】

势为天子不以尊贵骄人，富有天下不以财富欺人。

势为天子，未必贵也

A powerful emperor may not be high and noble.

势为天子，未必贵也；穷为匹夫，未必贱也。贵贱之分，在行之美恶。

《庄子·盗跖》

A powerful emperor may not be high and noble; a penniless man may not be humble and mean. What determines one's nobleness or meanness is how he behaves himself.

【注释】

作者借孔子弟子子张的话认为高低贵贱的区分不在地位而在行为之美恶。

【译文】

虽权势如天子，却未必尊贵；虽穷困如匹夫，却未必低贱；贵贱的区分，不在地位高低而在于行为的善恶。

水静则明烛须眉

Peaceful waters have a clear and level surface that gives an image.

水静则明烛须眉，平中准，大匠取法焉。

《庄子·天道》

Peaceful waters have a clear and level surface that gives an image of the beards and brows and offers a measure for the master carpenters.

【注释】

明烛：清楚地照到。烛，作动词，照。**平中（zhòng）准：**平到可以成为标准，今称水准。**大匠：**高明的木匠。**取法：**拿来作为效法的标准。高明的工匠衡量一个东西是否平，就是以水准为标准。

【译文】

水清静可以照见须眉，平到可以成为标准，为高明的木匠所效法。

水流乎无形

A stream of water runs without a fixed course from nowhere.

水流乎无形，发泄乎太清。

《庄子·列御寇》

A stream of water runs without a fixed course from nowhere and it flows toward the quiet nature.

【注释】

无形：没有固定的形迹，只是随地势而流。**发泄**：流露。**太清**：太虚之道，即自然之道。

【译文】

水流并没有固定的轨迹，纯粹出于自然随地势而流。

死生，命也，其有夜旦之常

Life and death are destined, just like the eternal succession.

死生，命也，其有夜旦之常，天也。人之有所不得与，皆物之情也。

《庄子·大宗师》

Life and death are destined, just like the eternal succession of day and night—they are both a natural course of events. Men do not have the power to control it: this is true of everything in the world.

【注释】

夜旦：白天，黑夜。常：永恒的现象。与：参与，干预。情：常情。

作者认为死生有命，日夜由天。这是自然的规律不是人为可以干预的。而且万物都不能例外。

【译文】

死生是命，如同日夜交替的永恒变化一样，是自然的规律。有许多事情是人力无法改变的，这是万物固有的常情。

天地者，万物之父母也

The Heaven and the Earth give birth to all the things in the world. The combination of the physical form and the vital energy results in the appearance of things.

天地者，万物之父母也，合则成体，散则成始。形精不亏，是谓能移。

《庄子·达生》

The Heaven and the Earth give birth to all the things in the world. The combination of the physical form and the vital energy results in the appearance of things; the separation of the physical form from the vital energy marks the beginning of new things. The perfect state of the physical form and the vital energy is called the "potential for transformation."

【注释】

天地者，万物之父母也：《至乐》篇："天无为以之清，地无为以之宁。故两无为相合，万物皆化生。"故说"天地者，万物之父母也"。合则成体：天地两无为交合则生成万物（包括人）的形体。散则成始：天地分离则万物各变为它的开始——返归于天地未分之时的混沌状态。能移：能随天地更生变化。

【译文】

天地是万物的父母，天地交合则生成万物的形体，天地分离则万物返归于混沌状态，形体健全而精神不亏，就能随天地更生变化。

天道运而无所积，故万物成

The natural course of events moves on and on so that everything in the world comes into existence.

天道运而无所积，故万物成；帝道运而无所积，故天下归；圣道运而无所积，故海内服。

《庄子·天道》

The natural course of events moves on and on so that everything in the world comes into existence; the emperors and kings follow Tao in their own way so that everyone in the world rallies around them; the sages follow Tao in their own way so that everyone within the four seas bows to them.

【注释】

天道：自然的规律。运：动。积：停滞。成：生成。归：归附。

庄子认为圣人虚静无为，任随万物不停的自然运动，故可以得天乐而王天下。

【译文】

天道不停地运行，万物得以生成；帝道不停地运行，天下所以归服；圣道不停地运行，所以海内宾服。

天与地无穷，人死者有时

The Heaven and the Earth are limitless whereas the human life is limited.

天与地无穷，人死者有时。操有时之具，而托于无穷之间，忽然无异骐骥之驰过隙也。不能说其志意，养其寿命者，皆非通道者也。

《庄子·盗跖》

The Heaven and the Earth are limitless whereas the human life is limited. One's limited life in the limitless Heaven and Earth vanishes as quickly as a horse galloping through a crevice. Whoever fails to please himself and to prolong his life knows no sensible truth.

【注释】

操：掌握。有时之具：指人的形体。无穷之间：指天地。

作者借盗跖的话说明：人生在世，如白驹过隙，故应以快活、长寿为目的。

【译文】

天地是无穷的，人的生命是有限的，将有限的生命寄托于无穷的天地之间，就像白驹过隙，不能随心所欲、保养其寿命的人，都不是通达于道的人。

天下有道，则与物皆昌

When the world is prevalent with Tao, he shares the prosperity with everything.

天下有道，则与物皆昌；天下无道，则修德就闲。

《庄子·天地》

When the world is prevalent with Tao, he shares the prosperity with everything; when the world is without Tao, he nurtures his own virtue and lives a seclusive life.

【注释】

昌：兴盛、成长。就闲：闲居。表示与世无争。

【译文】

天下有道，便与众同昌；天下无道，便闲居修德。

万物殊理，道不私

**Each of all the things in the world has its own laws,
but because Tao does not show partiality to any of them.**

万物殊理，道不私，故无名。无名故无为，无为而无不为。

《庄子·则阳》

Each of all the things in the world has its own laws，but because Tao does not show partiality to any of them，they are all nameless. He who is nameless does nothing；he who does nothing will accomplish anything.

【注释】

万物殊理，道不私： 大道是虚无抽象的，不会偏近于某一事物，因此不可名状，静寂无为。正因为无为，不干预万物，利于万物自然发展，故又是无所不为的。

【译文】

万物各有其理，道不偏私，所以无可名状。无可名状所以无为，无为而无不为。

万物职职，皆从无为殖

There are so many things in the world. Everything in the world is born with nothing having done anything.

万物职职，皆从无为殖。故曰天地无为也而无不为也，人也孰能得无为哉！

《庄子·至乐》

There are so many things in the world. Everything in the world is born with nothing having done anything. Therefore, as the saying goes, "The Heaven and the Earth do nothing and there is nothing they cannot do." However, who among the men can refrain from taking action?

【注释】

职职：繁多的样子。皆从无为殖：都是从两（天地）无为相交中繁殖出来的。殖，繁殖，产生。无为，指一清一宁。无不为：指能繁殖万物。人也孰能得无为哉：世俗之人只知有为不知无为，故作者感叹学得无为的人太少，感叹无为难得。

【译文】

万物繁多，都出自于无为。所以说天地无为而无不为，可惜懂得无为的人太少了！

为善无近名，为恶无近刑

When you do good, don't do it for the sake of fame.

为善无近名，为恶无近刑，缘督
以为经，可以保身，可以全生，可以
养亲，可以尽年。

《庄子·养生主》

When you do good, don't do it for the sake of fame;
when you do bad, don't do it as to incur punishment. If you
always keep to the proper way, you will be able to keep a
good health, preserve your nature, support your parents and
live out your full life span.

【注释】

名：名利。缘督：因顺自然。经：常，正道。亲：天性，精神。年：年寿，指
自然寿命。

作者认为富贵名誉和罪恶刑罚都是有害于养生的，因而主张做好事不追求名利，
做坏事不触犯刑罚，要走一条明哲保身的人生道路。

【译文】

做善事不追求名利，做不善事不要触犯刑罚，做事
顺其自然，就可以明哲保身，可以修身养性，可以高寿
善终。

闻在宥天下，不闻治天下也

I have heard of letting the world be and letting the world alone, but I have never heard of governing the world.

闻在宥天下，不闻治天下也。在之也者，恐天下之淫其性也；宥之也者，恐天下之迁其德也。天下不淫其性，不迁其德，有治天下者哉！

《庄子·在宥》

I have heard of letting the world be and letting the world alone, but I have never heard of governing the world. To let the world be is to fear that the world will go beyond its inborn nature; to let the world alone is to fear that the world will shift its virtue. If the world does not go beyond its inborn nature or shift its virtue, what is the need to govern the world?

【注释】

在宥（yòu）：自在宽容。在宥天下，意即任由天下万物的自然发展，不加人为的约束、促进作用。亦即庄子主张的以无为的态度对待天下。

【译文】

只听说任由天下自然发展，没听说过人为治理天下。人们自在，惟恐天下扰乱了他的本性；人们宽容，只恐天下改变了他的德性。天下不扰乱其本性，不改变其德性，何须治理天下。

无为为之之谓天

To act by doing nothing is called the way of the Heaven.

无为为之之谓天，无为言之之谓德，爱人利物之谓仁，不同同之之谓大，行不崖异之谓宽，有万不同之谓富。

《庄子·天地》

To act by doing nothing is called the way of the Heaven; to explain by saying nothing is called virtue; to love people and benefit things is called benevolence; to make dissimilar things similar is called greatness; to behave without absurdity or ostentation is called generosity; to embrace varieties of things is called wealth.

【注释】

爱人利物之谓仁：这里的"爱人利物"和儒家所说的"仁者爱人"墨家所说的"兼爱"等不同，他认为任随人与物本性的自然就是爱人利物了，而绝不是要对人对物表示亲爱。崖异：突出而区别于众。

【译文】

以无为的态度处世就是天道，以无为的方式去表述就是德，爱人利物就是仁，统一不同就是大，行为不表现出奇异就是宽，包容万物就是富。

无知无能者

No one can avoid what he does not know and what is beyond his power.

无知无能者，固人之所不免也。夫务免乎人之所不免者，岂不亦悲哉！至言去言，至为去为。齐知之，所知则浅矣。

《庄子·知北游》

No one can avoid what he does not know and what is beyond his power. Isn't it sad for men to try to avoid what is unavoidable? The perfect speech is absence of speech; the perfect action is absence of action. How shallow it is for men to equate personal knowledge with true knowledge!

【注释】

至言：合乎道的言论。**去言**：无言，不说。**至为**：合乎道的行为。**去为**：无为。齐：皆，全。

【译文】

有所不知有所不能，这本来是人所难免的。一定要避免人所难免的，岂不也很可悲吗？至言无言，至为无为。要是什么都知道，实际上所知的就很肤浅了。

吾生也有涯，而知也无涯

Man's life is limited but knowledge is unlimited.

吾生也有涯，而知也无涯，以有涯随无涯，殆已！

《庄子·养生主》

Man's life is limited but knowledge is unlimited. To pursue the unlimited with the limited is fatiguing.

【注释】

涯：限度。知：知识。随：追随。殆（dài）：疲困，危险。

作者认为为人处世要顺应自然，不求名利，不遭刑戮之害，这样就可以明哲保身，修身养性，就可以高寿善终。

【译文】

我们的生命是有限的，而知识是无限的，以有限的生命去追求无限的知识，必然会疲困不堪。

昔者庄周梦为胡蝶

I, by the name of Zhuang Zhou, once dreamed that I was a butterfly.

昔者庄周梦为胡蝶，栩栩然胡蝶也。自喻适志与！不知周也。俄然觉，则蘧蘧然周也。不知周之梦为胡蝶与？胡蝶之梦为周与？周与胡蝶则必有分矣。此之谓物化。

《庄子·齐物论》

I, by the name of Zhuang Zhou, once dreamed that I was a butterfly, a butterfly fluttering happily here and there. I was so pleased that I forgot that I was Zhuang Zhou. When I suddenly woke up, I was astonished to find that I was as a matter of fact Zhuang Zhou. Did Zhuang Zhou dream of the butterfly or did the butterfly dream of Zhuang Zhou? Between Zhuang Zhou and the butterfly there must be some distinctions. This is called "the transformation of things."

【注释】

栩栩（xǔ xǔ）：生动活泼。喻：知晓，觉得。适志：得意。不知周也：忘记了自己是庄周啊！蘧蘧（jù jù）：惊疑。梦醒之后，想到自己又是庄周，故感到惊奇而又可疑。物化：指物我界限消解，万物融化为一。

【译文】

从前庄周梦见自己变成了蝴蝶，一只生动活泼的蝴蝶，自己感觉得意洋洋，竟然忘记了自己是庄周。忽然梦醒了，惊疑之余才知道自己还是庄周。不知是庄周做梦化为蝴蝶呢？还是蝴蝶做梦化为庄周？庄周和蝴蝶必定有所分别的。这就是万物融化为一了。

西施病心而矉其里

The famous beauty Xi Shi frowned at neighbors when she had a heartache.

西施病心而矉其里，其里之丑人见之而美之，归亦捧心而矉其里。其里之富人见之，坚闭门而不出；贫人见之，挈妻子而去走。彼知矉美而不知矉之所以美。

《庄子·天运》

The famous beauty Xi Shi frowned at neighbors when she had a hertache. An ugly woman in her village thought that it made her beautiful, and so she returned home with her hands over her heart, also frowning at her neighbors. When the rich men in her village saw this, they would close the doors and stay at home. When the poor men say this, they would bring their wives and children and stay away from her. She knew that frowning was beautiful, but she did not know why it was beautiful.

【注释】
西施：古代美女，春秋越国人。病心：心痛。矉（Pín）：通颦，皱眉。里：居里，古时相传二十五家为一里。丑：面貌难看。捧心：捂着胸口。挈（qiè）：携带。

【译文】
西施心痛，常常皱着眉头，邻里的丑女看见了觉得她的样子很美，于是也手捂胸口皱着眉头。邻里的富人看见了，关紧大门而不出；穷人看见了，带着妻子儿女远走他乡。她只知道皱着眉头美，却不知皱眉头为什么美。

小惑易方，大惑易性。

A man with a mild confusion may change his direction of life; a man with a serious confusion may change his inborn nature.

小惑易方，大惑易性。

《庄子·骈拇》

A man with a mild confusion may change his direction of life; a man with a serious confusion may change his inborn nature.

【注释】

惑：疑惑，糊涂。**易**：变换，颠倒。**方**：方向。

庄子认为纯正的人性就是人自然的本性，而仁义不但不合人性，而且会伤性乱世。他说自从有虞氏标榜仁义扰乱天下，天下没有不奔命于仁义的。这不是用仁义来错乱本性吗？

【译文】

小糊涂会迷失方向，大糊涂则错失本性。

小知不及大知

Little learning does not come up to great learning.

小知不及大知，小年不及大年。

《庄子·逍遥游》

Little learning does not come up to great learning; the short-lived does not come up to the long-lived.

【注释】

知（zhì）：同"智"。不及：赶不上，比不上。年：寿命。小年、大年：短寿、长寿。

庄子认为"大知闲闲，小知间间。"（《齐物论》）意谓大智博而闲逸无为，小智精细而计较。是"小知不及大知"也。"朝菌不知晦朔，惠蛄不知春秋"。（《逍遥游》）意谓朝生暮死的菌子不可能知道一个月的时光，夏生秋死的蝉不可能知道一年的时光。是"小年不及大年"也。

【译文】

才智小不能理解才智大的，短命的不能了解长寿的。

孝子不谀其亲

A filial son who does not fawn upon his parents. . .

孝子不谀其亲，忠臣不谄其君，臣、子之盛也。

《庄子·天地》

A filial son who does not fawn upon his parents and a minister who does not flatter his lord have the best virtue of sons and ministers.

【注释】

谀（yú）：奉承。谄（chǎn）：讨好。盛：最。臣、子之盛：臣之最忠、子之最孝。

【译文】

孝子不奉承其父母，忠臣不谄媚其君主，这是臣之最忠，子之最孝的表现。

行贤而去自贤之行
If you are virtuous and do not think so. . .

行贤而去自贤之行，安往而不爱哉！

《庄子·山木》

If you are virtuous and do not think so, where would you go without being loved?

【注释】

阳子到宋国去，寄宿于旅店。店主人有两个妾，一个漂亮一个丑陋，丑陋的受尊宠而漂亮的被冷落。阳子问其中原因，旅店的主人说："漂亮的自以为漂亮，但我并不认为她漂亮；丑陋的自感丑陋，但我并不觉得她丑陋。"于是阳子对弟子们说了这句话。

庄子认为自我显耀则被人所贱，谦卑才能被人敬重。

【译文】

行为贤良而又不要自以为贤良，无论到哪里都会受到敬重。

养形必先之以物

For the nourishment of the physical form. . .

养形必先之以物，物有余而形不养者有之矣；有生必先无离形，形不离而生亡者有之矣。生之来不能却，其去不能止。

《庄子·达生》

For the nourishment of the physical form, certain things are needed; yet there are cases in which the physical form is not well nourished although a surplus of things is provided. For the preservation of life, it is of primary importance to prevent life from leaving the physical form; yet there are cases in which the physical form still exists although life no longer exists. The coming of life cannot be rejected while the going of life cannot be hindered.

【注释】

养形：保养身体。形，身体。**物**：物质条件，如衣食等。**离形**：即死亡。

【译文】

保养身体必须先有物质条件，但有的人虽然物质丰裕却保养不好身体；保有生命首先必须不脱离形体，但有的人虽然没有离开形体生命却已经死亡了。生命到来不能拒绝，离去无法挽留。

以德分人谓之圣

He who shares his virtue with others is called a sage.

以德分人谓之圣，以财分人谓之贤。以贤临人，未有得人者也；以贤下人，未有不得人者也。

《庄子·徐无鬼》

He who shares his virtue with others is called a sage and he who shares his talents with others is called a worthy man. A man who by his worth lords it over others will never win the support from others; a man who by his worth condescends over others will surely win the support from others.

【注释】

以德分人谓之圣：用自己的美德去影响别人的称得上圣人。**以贤临人**：标榜自己贤能，居高临下地对待别人。**以贤下人**：虽然自己贤能，但能谦逊待人。

【译文】

以自身美德影响别人的称为圣人，以自己财货施于别人的称为贤人。以贤能居高临下待人的，没有能得人心的；而贤能又谦逊待人的，没有不得人心的。

以富为是者，不能让禄

Those who strive for wealth will not give up their salary.

以富为是者，不能让禄；以显为是者，不能让名。亲权者，不能与人柄。

《庄子·天运》

Those who strive for wealth will not give up their salary; those who strive for reputation will not give up their good fame; and those who strive for power will not give up their position.

【注释】

是：善。**显**：显达，有名望。**亲权**：热衷于权势。**柄**：权位。

【译文】

以财富为追求目标的，便不会出让利禄；以荣显为追求目标的，便不会出让名誉；热衷于权势的，便不会以权位让人。

以瓦注者巧，以钩注者惮

The man will play with skill when he makes a bet with tiles.

以瓦注者巧，以钩注者惮，以黄金注者殙。其巧一也，而有所矜，则重外也。凡外重者内拙。

《庄子·达生》

The man will play with skill when he makes a bet with tiles; he will play with worry and care when he makes a bet with a silver buckle; he will lose his wits when he makes a bet with gold. His skill is the same, but his anxiety grows with the increasing value of his bet. Consideration of external things always disturbs people internally.

【注释】

以瓦注者巧：以瓦片作赌注，输了也只不过是瓦片，故心里没有负担。注，赌注。巧，轻巧。**钩**：带钩，一说银锞。**惮**：怕。**殙（hūn）**：心绪紊乱的样子。

【译文】

用瓦片作赌注心里没有负担，用银锞作赌注就有点紧张，用黄金作赌注则心神不定。他的赌技是一样的，但后者顾虑重重，这是由于注重身外之物的得失。注重于身外之物内心就会变得笨拙。

以虚静推于天地，通于万物

He applies his emptiness and peacefulness to the Heaven and the Earth, to everything in the world.

以虚静推于天地，通于万物，此之谓天乐。天乐者，圣人之心以畜天下也。

《庄子·天道》

He applies his emptiness and peacefulness to the Heaven and the Earth, to everything in the world. This is the so-called heavenly joy. Heavenly joy embodies the mind of the sage, with which he nourishes and governs the world.

【注释】

以虚静推于天地：对什么都要以虚静无为的态度对待。**圣人之心以畜天下：**圣人以天乐之心来管理天下，即所谓无为而治。

说明圣人虚静无为，任随万物不停的自然运动，故此可以得天乐而王天下。

【译文】

以虚静无为之心推及于天地之间，通达于万物，这就叫天乐。所谓天乐，就是以圣人之心管理天下，无为而治。

鱼处水而生，人处水而死

Fish can only survive in waters while men will die in waters.

鱼处水而生，人处水而死，彼必相与异，其好恶故异也。

《庄子·至乐》

Fish can only survive in waters while men will die in waters. As differences do exist between men and fish, they must have different likes and dislikes.

【注释】

彼必相与异： 人和鱼各自的生活特性不同。**故：** 通固，本来。

庄子认为种类不同，则好恶、本能亦不同。所以不能相互勉强或强加于人，而应当无为顺应自然。

【译文】

鱼在水里生龙活现，人在水里就会被淹死，两者的生活特性不同，好恶也就不同了。

鱼相造乎水，人相造乎道

As fish strive for water, so men strive for Tao.

鱼相造乎水，人相造乎道。相造乎水者，穿池而养给；相造乎道者，无事而生定。故曰鱼相忘乎江湖，人相忘乎道术。

《庄子·大宗师》

As fish strive for water, so men strive for Tao. To strive for water, the fish swim in the pond leading to rivers and lakes to get adequate nourishment; to strive for Tao, men do nothing to keep tranquil. Therefore, it is said, "As fish forget everything in rivers and lakes, so men forget everything in Tao."

【注释】

相造：适宜。穿池而养给：意谓离开水池，游到江湖去。穿，通过。无事而生定：无事，虚静。生，通性。生定，指心性恬淡，不为是非、爱憎所动。

【译文】

鱼适宜于水，人适宜于道。适宜水的，挖掘水池使通往江湖来供养；适宜道的，安息无事就天性自得。所以说，鱼游于江湖就忘记一切而自由快活，人游于道术就忘记一切而消遥自在。

朝菌不知晦朔，惠蛄不知春秋。

The fungi that sprout in the morning and die before evening do not know the alternation of night and day.

朝菌不知晦朔，惠蛄不知春秋。

《庄子·逍遥游》

The fungi that sprout in the morning and die before evening do not know the alternation of night and day; cicadas that are born in the spring and die in the summer or are born in the summer and die in the autumn do not know the alternation of spring and autumn.

【注释】

朝菌：一种朝生暮死的菌类植物。《释文》引司马彪曰："大芝也。天阴生粪上，见日则死。一名日及，故不知月之终始也。" **晦朔**：月终称晦，月初称朔。晦朔，一月也。 **惠蛄**（huì gū）：寒蝉，夏生秋死。 **春秋**：指一年。商代和周代前期一年只分春秋二季。寒蝉春生夏死，或夏生秋死，因此说它"不知春秋"。

【译文】

朝生暮死的菌子不会知道一个整月的时光，春生夏死或夏生秋死的寒蝉不会知道一整年的时光。

知道易，勿言难

It is not hard to understand Tao, but it is hard not to talk about it.

知道易，勿言难。知而不言，所以之天也；知而言之，所以之人也。古之人，天而不人。

《庄子·列御寇》

It is not hard to understand Tao, but it is hard not to talk about it. Understanding Tao but remaining silent about it is the path leading to the natural state; understanding Tao and bragging about it will take one to the secular world. The people in ancient times conformed themselves to the nature, and distanced themselves from conscious manipulation.

【注释】

之天：达到天的境界。之人：走人为之路。天而不人：奉行自然，不着人为。作者指出如果表现自己居功骄傲，得利忘形，就一定会给自己带来祸害。

【译文】

知道容易，知道而不说出来困难。知道而不说，可以达到自然的境界；知道而说出来，这是人为的举动。古人奉行自然而抛弃人为。

知其愚者，非大愚也

If they are aware that they are foolish，they are not
yet the worst fools.

知其愚者，非大愚也；知其惑者，非大惑也。大惑者，终身不解；大愚者，终身不灵。

《庄子·天地》

If they are aware that they are foolish, they are not yet the worst fools; if they are aware that they are confused, they are not yet in the worst confusion. Those who are in the worst confusion will never rid themselves of it all their lives; those who are the worst fools will never become clever all their lives.

【注释】

知其愚者，非大愚也：知道自己愚笨的，说明已经有点觉醒了，故说"非大愚也"。不解：不能解除迷惑，即不觉悟。不灵：不灵通。

【译文】

知道自己愚笨，就不算真愚笨；知道自己受迷惑，就不算真的迷惑。真正迷惑的人，终身不能觉悟；真正愚笨的人，终身不能通达。

知士无思虑之变则不乐

A man good at employing his wits is not happy when he does not see the chances to develop his thoughts.

知士无思虑之变则不乐，辩士无谈说之序则不乐，察士无凌谇之事则不乐，皆囿于物者也。

《庄子·徐无鬼》

A man good at employing his wits is not happy when he does not see the chances to develop his thoughts; a man good at debates is not happy when he does not find the opportunity to display his eloquence; a man good at picking mistakes is not happy when he does not have a chance to vent his reproaches. They are all confined by external things.

【注释】

思虑之变：指考虑问题灵活，多方设法。谈说之序：指论说的逻辑性。序，层次。察士：以明察见长的人。他们善于发现问题，所以往往能抓住别人的毛病。凌谇（suì）：言辞尖锐，凌辱责骂。皆囿于物者也：指上述几种人都是被名利之类的东西所局限。囿（yòu），局限，束缚。

【译文】

智谋之士喜欢思虑多变，善辩之士喜欢言谈的逻辑有序，明察之士喜欢言辞尖锐，他们都被外在事物所束缚。

知天乐者，其生也天行

He who understands heavenly joy follows nature when he is alive.

知天乐者，其生也天行，其死也物化。静而与阴同德，动而与阳同波。故知天乐者，无天怨，无人非，无物累，无鬼责。

《庄子·天道》

He who understands heavenly joy follows nature when he is alive, changes with everything in the world when he is dead, shares the virtue of yin when he is still, and shares the movement with yang when he is active. Therefore, he who understands heavenly joy will not complained by the Heaven, will not be blamed by men, will not be entangled in worldly affairs, and will not be reproached by ghosts or spirits.

【注释】

天行：自然的运动，即生是自然运动的结果。物化：事物的转化，即死是事物的一种转化。同波：合流。

【译文】

知天乐的人，他生是顺乎自然而运行，死是事物的转化。静则与阴同德，动则与阳合流（一静一动都与阴阳合拍）。所以知天乐的人，不怨天，不尤人，没有外物牵累，没有鬼神责罚。

知天之所为，知人之所为者

To know what the Heaven can do and to know what man can do—that is the ultimate human knowledge.

庄子说

知天之所为，知人之所为者，至矣。知天之所为者，天而生也；知人之所为者，以其知之所知以养其知之所不知，终其天年而不中道天者，是知之盛也。

《庄子·大宗师》

To know what the Heaven can do and to know what man can do—that is the ultimate human knowledge. To know what the Heaven can do is to know that everything comes from the Heaven. To know what man can do is to use one's knowledge of the known to nourish his knowledge of the unknown against premature death until his natural death. That is the summit of human knowledge.

【注释】

知：懂得，知道。所为：作用。至：极至，顶点。天而生：自然而产生。盛：至。

【译文】

懂得天的作用，懂得人的作用，其知识就算到顶了。懂得天，就是懂得宇宙万物是天所生的；懂得人，就是知道按照自己的能力办事，不渴求自己不懂的东西，以保持长寿，这是最聪明的。

知足者，不以利自累也

He who is content with what he has will not exhaust himself for any high position and handsome pay.

知足者，不以利自累也；审自得者，失之而不惧；行修于内者，无位而不怍。

《庄子·让王》

He who is content with what he has will not exhaust himself for any high position and handsome pay; he who leads a peaceful and carefree existence will not worry about any loss; he who persists in cultivating his mind will not feel ashamed for his humble and low position.

【注释】

审自得者：对于自己的得失看得很清楚的人。审，明察。行修于内：进行内心的精神修养。位：官爵。怍（zuò）：惭愧。

【译文】

知足的人，不因利禄而拖累自己；有自知之明的人，不忧惧失去什么；修养内心的人，不因无官爵而惭愧。

直木先伐，甘井先竭。

A straight tree is the first to be cut down; and a sweet well is the first to be drawn dry.

直木先伐，甘井先竭。

《庄子·山木》

A straight tree is the first to be cut down; and a sweet well is the first to be drawn dry.

【注释】

直木先伐：直木有用，故易被人先砍伐。**甘井先竭**：甘美的井水，人人来取，故先枯竭。

庄子认为有用（即成材）有害，他还认为成材为患，不成材也为患，不得已的话，只好处于材与不材之间。而处于材与不材之间也会难免带来拖累的，只有游于无为的道德境界才是最理想的。

【译文】

笔直（有用）的树木先遭砍伐，甘美的井水最先被取尽。

至乐活身，唯无为几存

In refrainment of action we are closest to perfect happiness and enjoyment of life.

至乐活身，唯无为几存。请尝试言之：天无为以之清，地无为以之宁，故两无为相合，万物皆化生。

《庄子·至乐》

In refrainment of action we are closest to perfect happiness and enjoyment of life. I shall try to put it this way. The Heaven is clear because it does nothing; the Earth is quiet because it does nothing. As neither the Heaven nor the Earth does anything, everything in the world is born out of them.

【注释】

至乐活身：只有无为接近于活身之道。几存：接近。天无为以之清：无为之道又叫"一"，即绝对的统一，没有矛盾斗争，故天地因此而清静。以，因。见《老子》："天得一以清，地得一以宁。"

【译文】

至乐可以活身，而只有无为接近于至乐活身之道。请让我试着说明这一点：天因无为而清虚，地因无为而宁静，这两种无为相结合，从而使万物变化生长。

褚小者不可以怀大

A small bag cannot hold large things.

褚小者不可以怀大，绠短者不可以汲深。

《庄子·至乐》

A small bag cannot hold large things; and a short rope cannot reach a deep well.

【注释】

褚（zhǔ）：袋子。怀：装。绠（gěng）：吊水用的绳子。

这是孔子引管子的两句话，可是却不见于今本《管子》，其实这是庄子借孔子之口说出的话。意谓不能相互勉强或强加于人，而应无为而顺其自然。

【译文】

小袋子不能装大东西，短绳子不能从深井里汲水。

朱泙漫学屠龙 （屠龙之技）

Zhu Pingman spent a fortune in learning the skill of killing dragons from Zhili Yi.

朱泙漫学屠龙于支离益，单千金
之家，三年技成而无所用其巧。

《庄子·列御寇》

Zhu Pingman spent a fortune in learning the skill of killing dragons from Zhili Yi. Three years later he acquired the skill. But he found no opportunity to practise the skill, as there is no dragon in the world.

【注释】

朱泙（pèng）漫、支离益：都是虚拟的人物。单：通"殚"，尽。家：家产。巧：指屠龙的技巧。

【译文】

朱泙漫跟支离益学屠龙，耗尽千金家产，用了三年的时间，但学成后却没有机会运用他的屠龙技巧。（因为世上根本没有龙）

庄子与惠子游于濠梁之上

Zhuang Zi travelled with Hui Zi over a bridge on the Hao River.

庄子与惠子游于濠梁之上。庄子曰："儵鱼出游从容，是鱼之乐也。"惠子曰："子非鱼，安知鱼之乐？"庄子曰："子非我，安知我不知鱼之乐？"

《庄子·秋水》

Zhuang Zi travelled with Hui Zi over a bridge on the Hao River. Zhuang Zi said, "The fish is swimming at ease. This is how the fish enjoy themselves." Hui Zi said, "You are not a fish. How do you know the fish are enjoying themselves?" Zhuang Zi said, "You are not me. How do you know I don't know about the fish?"

【注释】

濠（háo）梁：濠，水名，在今安徽凤阳县附近。梁，拦河堰。儵（tiáo）鱼：白色，俗称苍条鱼。

庄子在这里用偷换概念的手法进行诡辩，惠子本来问的是"你怎么知道鱼快乐呢？"庄子变成了"你从哪儿知道鱼快乐呢？"庄子把所问问题变成了地点。

【译文】

庄子和惠施在濠水的河堰上游玩。庄子说："小白鱼自由自在地游来游去，这是鱼的快乐。"

惠施说："你又不是鱼，怎么会知道鱼的快乐？"

庄子说："你又不是我，怎么知道我不知道鱼的快乐？"

图书在版编目（CIP）数据

庄子说／蔡希勤编注．—北京：华语教学出版社，2006
（中国圣人文化丛书．老人家说系列）
ISBN 7 - 80200 - 213 - 3

Ⅰ．庄…　Ⅱ．蔡…　Ⅲ．汉语—对外汉语教学—语言读物　Ⅳ. H195. 5

中国版本图书馆 CIP 数据核字（2006）第 071861 号

出 版 人：单　瑛
责任编辑：韩　晖　　封面设计：胡　湖
印刷监制：佟汉冬　　插图绘制：李士伋

老人家说·庄子说
蔡希勤　编注

*

©华语教学出版社
华语教学出版社出版
（中国北京百万庄大街 24 号　邮政编码 100037）
电话：(86)10 - 68995871
传真：(86)10 - 68326333
网址：www. sinolingua. com. cn
电子信箱：hyjx@ sinolingua. com. cn
北京松源印刷有限公司印刷
中国国际图书贸易总公司海外发行
（中国北京车公庄西路 35 号）
北京邮政信箱第 399 号　邮政编码 100044
新华书店国内发行
2006 年（大 32 开）第一版
2006 年第一版第一次印刷
（汉英）
ISBN 7 - 80200 - 213 - 3
9 - CE - 3730P
定价：29. 80